IN BAD FAITH

ANDREW
LEVINE

IN BAD FAITH

What's Wrong

with the

Opium of

the People

Prometheus Books

59 John Glenn Drive
Amherst, New York 14228–2119

Published 2011 by Prometheus Books

Cover art © 2005 Pepin van Roojen
Cover design by Grace M. Conti-Zilsberger

Inquiries should be addressed to

Prometheus Books
59 John Glenn Drive
Amherst, New York 14228–2119
VOICE: 716–691–0133
FAX: 716–691–0137
WWW.PROMETHEUSBOOKS.COM

15 14 13 12 11   5 4 3 2 1

Library of Congress Cataloging-in-Publication Data

Levine, Andrew, 1944–
    In bad faith : what's wrong with the opium of the people / By Andrew Levine.
        p. cm.
    Includes bibliographical references.
    ISBN 978–1–61614–470–8 (pbk. : alk. paper)
    ISBN 978–1–61614–471–5 (ebook)
    1. Religion—Philosophy. 2. Belief and doubt. 3. Faith. I. Title.

BL51.L48 2011
210—dc23   2011023931

CONTENTS

PREFACE

My dealings with Christianity and Islam, and even with Judaism, have been mainly cerebral. I was raised in a post–World War II, suburban, upper middle class, nonobservant Jewish household. Like all my Jewish friends, I was sent to Hebrew School and, at age thirteen, had a Bar Mitzvah. Then, not of my choosing, my Jewish education continued for another year or two at our conservative (but hardly traditional) "temple." I never took that so-called education seriously and, like my schoolmates, I learned almost nothing. Then, thanks to an odd confluence of circumstances, at the age of sixteen, I rebelled into traditional Judaism or rather into the version of it that I could construct from reading and from attendance at a nearby synagogue which, though conservative, was more traditional than the one to which I had been sent. Even there, however, I had little contact with the real deal. Judaism, for me then, was largely what I imagined it to be. I went to Columbia University in New York City, partly because of its proximity to the Jewish Theological Seminary, a center of modern, but still traditional, Jewish learning. It didn't take long in that milieu, where the real deal was much in evidence, for me to become disabused. I have never looked back.

In partial mitigation for this adolescent lapse, I would

note, with regard to what I now find especially deplorable about it, that it took place before Zionists hijacked the religion completely. In retrospect, I can see anticipations that this was about to happen in what I remember from what we were made to read in those post–Bar Mitzvah classes. But, before Israel's game-changing 1967 War, the problems inherent in fusing faith with support for an ethnocratic settler state were not nearly so apparent as they have since become; especially not to a politically unsophisticated teenager. I would add too that, at an intellectual level, the books I read and the practices with which I became acquainted were indeed of great interest. Like their Christian and Islamic counterparts, they remain, for me, a source of endless fascination.

At Columbia, a course called "Contemporary Civilization" was part of the core curriculum. Despite the name, there was nothing contemporary about it. In the first year, we read and discussed bits and snippets from the classics of Western intellectual history—from Greco-Roman antiquity through the French Revolution. Needless to say, in a course that ranged over so much material, there could be very little opportunity for deep thinking of the kind philosophers do, or claim to do; in effect and (I suppose) by intent, the course was a means for installing a shared cultural literacy. It performed that function well. The quip was that "CC," as we called it, was where atheists taught Jews about Christianity. There was something to that—not just descriptively but also pedagogically. To this day, I believe that to gain a sound purchase on "faith perspectives," to make sense of them, we can learn the most from those who have none.

From that time on, I have read a good deal more about Judaism and Christianity and, in recent years, Islam. But my grasp of these religious traditions, including the one into which I was born, hardly qualifies as scholarly. I have been and still am a political philosopher—a worker in a different bailiwick. This too provides a perspective that can be illuminating. That was the idea in CC and in "Humanities A," its companion course on world (Western) literature. In CC, I was taught by an economist in the first semester and a political theorist in the second. My Humanities teacher was an English professor. They had to work through material not in their bailiwicks too. That can be a good thing when the point is to convey a general sense of what is going on; it certainly was in my experience. Experts would have had to simplify; and, in this age of hyperspecialization, they often lack the requisite mastery of their respective fields to provide genuinely magisterial accounts of them. Scholars obliged to talk about fields that are not their own have to rely more on their wits. They are therefore well positioned to see the forest for the trees, and sometimes they do.

At the University of Wisconsin, where I taught philosophy for many years, the norm was to teach one lower-level undergraduate course each semester, along with a graduate or upper-level undergraduate course in one's specialty. Thus I spent many a semester teaching introductory philosophy where the question "Does God exist?" is a staple. Beyond that, I purposefully avoided anything smacking of philosophy of religion. But I inherited a course called "Man (later "Humanity"), Religion and Society," which, on the grounds that it is best to teach about what one knows, I turned into a course in social theory, albeit with a focus on religion. Thus, for many years, I taught Feuerbach, Durkheim, Freud, and Nietzsche, the authors I discuss in what follows here.

As a philosopher, I have worked on problems in contemporary political philosophy, and on historical figures— especially Jean-Jacques Rousseau and Thomas Hobbes. However, my main interest has been in Marx and Marxism. While still a graduate student and for about ten years thereafter, I approached Marx largely from the perspective provided by the French Marxist Louis Althusser. Thereafter my work fell more into the emerging fold of "analytical Marxism," though I always remained somewhat peripheral to the core of that movement.[1] However what I have to say about Feuerbach, a major influence on Marx's early writings, is shaped mainly by Althusserian understandings. My Althusserian interests also led me to read or reread Freud and to engage Freudian theory. I would note, however, that, for me, Althusserianism, much like my adolescent encounter with Judaism, was at least partly something I figured out on my own. When I encountered real Althusserians, I became similarly disabused.

From time to time, I also taught courses in social theory in which I developed an interest in Durkheim's work. I have had a love–hate relationship with Nietzsche's work since my lapse into Judaism days. For most of my time as a professional philosopher, Nietzsche was a despised figure, at least in the circles in which I traveled. Lately, the tide seems to have turned. In any case, I have been an enthusiastic reader of his for many years.

As a political philosopher, it eventually dawned on me that the main puzzle politics poses, at least at this point in history, is not so much what ought to be the case as why it is not. Throughout my time as a political philosopher, the main figure shaping the intellectual terrain was John Rawls. There is much that can be said in defense of this focus, and much that can be said about its shortcomings.[2] But one thing is very clear: there is an air of unreality to Rawlsian liberalism. Nowhere is this more evident than in the ventures his work has inspired in normative democratic theory, where a model of civil and reasonable deliberation conflicts starkly with the reality of real-world politics.

But however that may be, by standing on his shoulders and those of the giants of modern political thought, along with many lesser thinkers as well, it is clear enough what ought to be in the political realm. To be sure, since political philosophy inevitably bears some relation to real-world politics, there will always be obstinate defenders of what is obviously mistaken. Libertarianism, or at least the kind that "conservatives" favor, is an example. Among theologians and philosophers of religion, there is an even more obdurate desire to defend the indefensible. Nevertheless, as the authors I discuss knew well, the interesting questions with regard to religion too have little or nothing to do with what ought to be. They have to do with why there is so much resistance to the obvious, with what we should make of this sorry state of affairs, and with what we should do to change it.

It is said that it is good manners to avoid religious *and* political topics in polite conversation, presumably because both subjects are contentious and therefore divisive. But in fact, at the level at which most ordinary conversation proceeds, there is nothing that *ought* to be contentious or divisive. In both cases, we are in the realm of the obvious. Yet, hardly anyone seems to notice. This is a remarkable state of affairs, and it does indeed beg for an explanation.

The authors I will discuss engage this problem at a level that resonates with important departures in psychology, social theory, and philosophy. But there is also a superficial reason why the obviously indefensible persists that is so commonplace that it is almost always overlooked. I have in mind the sheer inertia of human thought. We all of us some of the time, and some of us all of the time, simple-mindedly accept what we are persistently told; and we all resist taking account of evidence that runs counter to our beliefs. How often, when calamities strike, do survivors thank God for their good fortune, finding 'proof' in their condition that a beneficent God is real? It would be unkind, and far too easy, to ask them how, if they are believers, they account for the misfortunes for which they thank God for relief. Why is there such blindness to the incontrovertible conclusion that if God exists, he must be a sadist or an incompetent or both? Why is such willful blindness so difficult to expunge? My wonderment about the pervasive obtuseness that has become a condition for the possibility of Judaism's, Christianity's, and Islam's survival motivates the inquiry that follows and serves as its point of departure.

INTRODUCTION

That greater and lesser evils have always been with us ought to be a problem for believers in an all-powerful, all-knowing, and perfectly good God; and since evils differ from the ordinary burdens of existence only in magnitude, not in kind, daily experience raises the problem continually and relentlessly. One would therefore expect believers to protest against God's sadism or at least to concede that God has much to answer for. However, the faithful seldom inveigh against the Creator. Fearful of holding him to account or oblivious to the horrors around them or blind to the conflict between their beliefs and the facts on the ground, they acquiesce, accepting it all without complaint.[1]

Remarkable as this may be, those who hold God blameless are nevertheless in the right. To be blameworthy, God would have to exist; and that he does not. Therefore, he can hardly be condemned, except in an ironic sense or in a manner of speaking.

But *faith* in God can be condemned. It can be condemned for the harms it causes, but I will not have much to say about that here. What I have in mind has more to do with faith's character than its consequences. The authors I will discuss contributed toward developing a normative standard according to which people who hold beliefs that they know, or should know, are unworthy of serious consideration are in what I will call *bad faith*. My claim is that, in the modern age, for all but the most benighted among us, faith in God runs afoul of this charge.

To be clear, what I have in mind are so-called faith perspectives; I have no quarrel with the epistemic stance the word "faith" sometimes describes. When "faith" just means confidence in beliefs that are neither disproved nor sustained by compelling arguments, there is seldom anything to fault. Faith in this sense is often unavoidable and usually unobjectionable; it may even be desirable when the alternatives are indecisiveness or indifference. What is objectionable is faith in God; the kind of faith adherents of the so-called Abrahamic religions—Judaism, Christianity, and Islam—evince.

I will assume without argument that, despite their many differences, these religions are enough alike to be accused of the same failing. The term "Abrahamic" asserts this commonality. I will have nothing to say about what the actual views of the patriarch Abraham might have been, nor will I even speculate as to whether anyone like the figure depicted in the Bible and Koran ever existed. The Abrahamic religions came into being centuries after Abraham is supposed to have lived; they, not Abraham, are the issue here. These religions claim that there is one and only one God, the God of Abraham, Isaac, and Jacob, his son and grandson, and they ascribe a foundational role to Abraham's covenant with this supreme being. It will be convenient to suspend disbelief by taking these self-representations at their word. In claiming a common genealogy, Judaism, Christianity, and Islam acknowledge a common set of core beliefs. On this, they are not mistaken.

* * *

The first philosopher to use "bad faith" (*mauvais foi*) in roughly the sense I have in mind was Jean-Paul Sartre. However, Sartre did not directly connect the concept with belief in God. He was mainly concerned with other problems—especially the mind's capacity for self-deception and its implications for human freedom. Faith in God surely does involve self-deception. But I will be more concerned with people holding beliefs they should reject than with how they deceive themselves into believing as they do. Sartre's claim, operationalized and applied to Abrahamic religiosity, turns into an empirical hypothesis: that some (perhaps most) people who profess faith in God *really* don't believe what they think they do. I agree mainly because I cannot fathom how otherwise reasonable people could be believers. But I cannot prove that believers are deceiving themselves—not only because empirical hypotheses require evidence, evidence that no one has, but also because it is unclear how such evidence could be obtained. It is also relevant that Sartre's usage differs from colloquial and legal understandings of "bad faith." In ordinary speech and in the law, the expression implies willful disingenuity; those who act in bad faith intend to deceive. This is not the case with most believers; self-deceived or not, they are *sincere*.

Still, Sartrean "bad faith" is of a piece with the view I will develop. But inasmuch as the connection is indirect and vague, rather than drawing on Sartre, I will mine the work of four nineteenth- and early twentieth-century thinkers— Ludwig Feuerbach, Émile Durkheim, Sigmund Freud, and Friedrich Nietzsche. Neither Durkheim nor Freud nor even Nietzsche, who zealously denigrated Judaism and Christianity, are known mainly for their views on religion; Feuerbach is the exception. However, they all dealt with the topic in writings that have become classics of philosophical criticism, social theory, and psychology. Working through what they wrote with a view to teasing out the notion of bad faith I have in mind provides a purchase on key aspects of their thought. This is worth doing in its own right. But, for the present purpose, gaining a better understanding of their thinking is a side-benefit. The point is to glean insights that clarify what is wrong with Abrahamic religiosity.

For the most part, I will neither criticize nor endorse the views these authors advance, nor will I have much to say about the theoretical frameworks within which they operate. Doing so would be a distraction. But I will say enough to present each author's positions sympathetically. In some instances, their views will seem incompatible; sometimes they really are, though seldom as much as may appear. But, in a very general way, these thinkers agree on what theistic faith is about and therefore on how, in general, to make sense of it. More importantly, in working out their respective explanations, each of them contributed to the development of the standard against which faith stands indicted.

Each of the authors I will discuss believed that, because we are reflective beings, we cannot abide a meaningless existence, and that this fact of human nature, joined with a universal human capacity for constructing meanings, accounts for religion's ubiquity and durability. They also believed that humankind can rise above faith in God or gods. And they each wondered why modern men and women had not done so long ago. They therefore each set out to account for the persistence of the idea that God exists.

In recent years, a few investigators, drawing on work in cognitive psychology and evolutionary anthropology, have broached these questions too.[2] The results of their inquiries are too underdeveloped to speak of a settled "paradigm" or even a consensus view, but it is fair to say that the idea guiding their research is that natural selection has favored the development in human populations of mental structures that identify *agency* not just in other persons or in animal predators and quarry, but also in things in general including unseen (and unseeable) things. This suggests that we are "hardwired," as it were, to find agency everywhere, even when there is none to find; and that we are therefore disposed to believe in *supernatural* agents, beings that exist outside nature but that somehow act in the natural world.

Whether or not this hypothesis is compatible with positions taken by Feuerbach, Durkheim, Freud and Nietzsche, it points in a different direction. It suggests that faith perspectives may be more difficult to eradicate than our authors believed. Were there not abundant evidence to the contrary, it might even be thought to imply that it is humanly impossible not to believe in God. This marks an important difference. Each of the authors I will discuss envisioned *freedom from* religion as a goal, and they each thought that their respective explanatory projects can have emancipatory consequences. Research agendas that emphasize powerfully constraining mental or biological causes do not have similar implications.

Although my focus will move from Feuerbach to Durkheim to Freud and then back to Nietzsche, my aim is not to concoct a story about the emergence of an idea or set of ideas that draws on the successive contributions of these thinkers. There is no story to tell, if only because their points of agreement are so general and because the theoretical frameworks in which they operate are so diverse. My aim instead is to establish the cogency and plausibility of a diffuse but nevertheless cohesive explanatory and normative project—one that indicts the Abrahamic religions on grounds of bad faith.

*   *   *

The four very different thinkers whose work I will discuss shared a puzzlement that none of them formulated explicitly, though Freud came closest. In effect, they agreed that the main question Abrahamic (and perhaps other) religions pose for people living in a modern, secular culture is why they still exist at all. Why do they survive and even flourish, when the beliefs they uphold, beliefs that justify their existence, fail to pass muster according to standards that have become the norm in other aspects of life?

The Abrahamic religions vary in the degree of importance they attach to beliefs. Christianity is at one end of the spectrum; throughout its history and in nearly all its varieties, it has emphasized doctrinal correctness. Judaism is at the other extreme; although Jews in premodern times and some orthodox Jews today believe in the literal truth of Old Testament stories, Judaism itself has generally been undemanding in matters of doctrinal conviction. Islam occupies a middle ground; the beliefs it insists upon are few in number but essential. On the other hand, until modern times, Judaism has been extremely demanding with respect to the observance of rituals and laws. To this day, *orthodoxy* in a Jewish context does not mean right belief, as the name suggests, but right practice. Christianity has been remarkably undemanding in this respect. From the time it began to break away from Judaism, Christian authorities were willing to permit and sometimes even to encourage local customs, mores, and traditions that are not directly at odds with Christian beliefs. As in Judaism, Islam's laws regulate nearly every aspect of life. For understanding the Abrahamic religions, especially Judaism and Islam, it can therefore be misleading to focus on beliefs more than laws, rituals, and practices. But this is what I shall do. This is appropriate inasmuch as I aim to defend the claim that to profess allegiance to the any of the Abrahamic religions in modern times is to be in bad faith. Jews, Christians, and Muslims are at fault because of what they profess to believe.

*   *   *

The idea that God exists, *theism*, is a foundational claim in all the Abrahamic religions. Each of the authors I will discuss took for granted that this belief is untenable, and that the issue has been settled philosophically at least since the eighteenth century. I agree. I will presently rehearse some long-established arguments that support this conclusion.

Strictly speaking, the arguments that undo belief in God's existence are directed not at theism, but at what eighteenth century thinkers called *deism*. Deists believe that there exists an omnipotent, omniscient, perfectly good being who is the creator of all that is. Theists add the idea that this being takes a direct interest in what goes on in his creation—or at least with an infinitesimally small part of it, the human part. Theists believe that God intervenes in human affairs through miracles or by answering prayers or by bestowing favors or hardships according to his will, or at least by shaping the course of human history. Theists also claim that human beings can have a personal relationship with the creator of the universe.

Because the being deists, and therefore theists, believe in is supposed to have created all there is, and because it would be pointless, if not illogical, to multiply creators beyond necessity or to imagine additional noncreative omnipotent, omniscient, and perfectly good Beings, theists are *monotheists*; they believe that God is One. Before monotheism became established, most pastoral peoples were *polytheists*; they believed that godly or godlike (theistic) powers were divided among a number of immortal, though imperfect, Beings. Some hunters and gatherers were polytheists too. Others believed in "spirits"—beings with humanlike personalities but without sufficient powers to count as full-fledged gods. Because these peoples lacked the distinction between the *nat-*

ural and the *supernatural*—in other words, because they lacked a concept of nature—the spirits they worshiped were gods or protogods only in retrospect. To believers, they were simple presences in the way that stones, trees, and rivers are for us.

The Abrahamic religions are monotheistic—though, in the case of Christianity, fine arguing is needed to reconcile monotheism with the doctrine of the Trinity. But Abrahamic faith and monotheism are not quite the same. There have been full-fledged monotheistic religions that are not Abrahamic; Zoroastrianism is an example. And, by most accounts, monotheism was not an Abrahamic invention. The idea appears to be of Egyptian origin, though it may also have arisen independently in Persia and among pastoral peoples in the Near East during the late Bronze Age. Although there is little evidence to support the claim and mounting evidence against it, the conventional view is that Egyptian monotheism took root among the Pharaoh's Hebrew slaves. This is probably more fiction than fact. It is far from clear even that the ancient Israelites ever were slaves in Egypt or, if they were, that the story of the exodus has any historical grounding. But even allowing that the Biblical account is generally correct, it is worth noting that, according to it, it required centuries for a robust monotheism to become secure in ancient Israel. As remarked, it is far from clear how secure it is even today within Christianity.

Nowadays, Abrahamic monotheism affects nearly everyone on earth. Once Christianity became the official religion of the Roman Empire in the fourth century of the Common Era, it spread, over the centuries that followed, throughout much of the Eurasian landmass from the Atlantic Ocean to the interior of the Indian subcontinent. Then, thanks to European colonialism, its reach expanded into the Americas, Australasia, and Africa. Arab conquests spread Islam into many formerly Christian lands, but Islam also took root in previously unaffected quarters in Africa, southern and eastern Asia, Oceana, and, of course, throughout the Middle East. In China and Japan, and in Southeast Asia, neither Islam nor Christianity ever became dominant. But they have long existed in that part of the world, and their ways of thinking have spilled over into the indigenous religious traditions found there.

Abrahamic monotheism has therefore shaped the political life of our planet for a very long time. If there were a God to thank, we should thank him heartily for the fact that, in the modern era, with the slow but inexorable onset of enlightenment and secularism, its influence has waned. However, lately, the current appears to have shifted. The old religions, regarded as plain anachronisms in historically Jewish, Christian, and Islamic communities only decades ago, have reemerged as poles of attraction for many of the world's peoples. I would suggest that this step backwards is a reaction to the setbacks suffered in recent decades by the agents of progressive change. But it could also be that an inexorable irrationality inherent in human nature has lately reasserted itself. The authors I will discuss shed light on both prospects and on the relation between them.

*   *   *

Those authors are as different as can be, in ways both obvious and subtle. Nevertheless, it is understandable that they would have unwittingly joined together in advancing a common normative standard. The idea is inherent in their respective explanatory projects, and the puzzlement that motivates them. Some of those projects—Feuerbach's most clearly, but also Freud's and Nietzsche's—imply the urgency of moving from bad faith to good, where *good faith* retrieves bad faith's effect without its meretricious doctrinal convictions. Durkheim stood in an intellectual tradition that insisted on an unbridgeable gap between value judgments and scientific explanations. But one cannot read what Durkheim wrote about religion without concluding that the value judgments he made were of a piece with those of the others, even if he did not think that they followed from his scientific work. He opposed bad faith for roughly the same reason as the others, and, even more clearly than Freud or Nietzsche, supported the kind of good faith Feuerbach envisioned.

Is *good faith* possible? Put differently: Can we retrieve what is worth retaining in theism while denying the existence of God? Feuerbach believed not only in the possibility of good faith but also in its imminent emergence. Despite their vast theoretical and political differences, Durkheim held a similar view. He did not share Feuerbach's conviction that bad faith would shortly give way to good, but he did think that something like what Feuerbach had in mind is in humanity's future. Implicitly, Freud thought so too.

Nietzsche agreed as well, though he envisioned a more profound transformation in consciousness than the others; one for which the obverse of Abrahamic religiosity would be only a transitional phase. What Nietzsche imagined is a world *beyond* good and bad faith; a world in which the opposition Feuerbach emphasized is superseded altogether. This would not be the first time that a type of faith was superseded. For almost two millennia, no one has cared whether, say, ancient Roman beliefs were true. It has been taken for granted that they are not; and the world has moved on. Nietzsche envisioned a time when the same would be true of faith in the God of Abraham, Isaac, and Jacob; a time when theism would no longer matter and therefore neither would atheism in the sense that it mattered for heirs of the Enlightenment tradition. Feuerbach, Durkheim, and Freud subscribed to a similar vision. But, unlike Nietzsche, none of them had much to say about the prospect, perhaps because the fact that humankind is not yet anywhere near that goal weighed too heavily upon them. Nietzsche sometimes wrote prophetically as if "the death of God" was already an accomplished fact. But, for all his bluster, he agreed with the others on the difficulties in the way of making that vision real. He was more dramatic than they were and more focused on the end, but he was not of a different mind.

*   *   *

We are, however, a long way from good faith, much less from reaching the destination Nietzsche prophesied. This unfortunate fact bears on a problem none of our authors addressed. Since the French Revolution, political forces have arrayed themselves notionally and, for the most part, actually on a

Left–Right spectrum, where the Left is the party of progress and the Right of tradition and order. The Left has had and still has liberal and socialist wings, and it can be reformist or revolutionary. It has been comprised of nearly as many opposing sects as any Abrahamic religion except perhaps Protestant Christianity. But a common point of agreement, particularly in the nineteenth century, was that to be for progress is to oppose secular and clerical authority, and therefore also the religions that reigning clerisies and their counterparts in the political regime promote.

Feuerbach was the only one of the authors I will discuss who identified unequivocally with the Left; in Germany in the 1830s and '40s, he was a leading figure in its revolutionary wing. Durkheim was a liberal, though his interests were more theoretical than political. Much the same can be said of Freud. Nietzsche, the least political of the four, was adopted long ago by the Right, though there are liberals who would claim him, too. Thus, the authors I discuss were hardly of one mind on politics. But, along with most of their contemporaries, they would have agreed that the idea of a religious Left is, if not oxymoronic, then at least highly problematic. Few think so today. Decades before the socialist movement fell into the crisis from which it has yet to recover, a religious Left took shape, dispatching the idea that anything of the sort is unthinkable. This is a remarkable phenomenon, almost as remarkable as the persistence of faith itself. When, in the final chapters of this book, I ponder how this came about, I will show that these two hard-to-account-for developments are not as independent of one another as one might think.

I will argue that militants of the religious Left are Young Hegelian atheists without knowing it. I will argue too that, despite all they do to implement Left ideals, even they are blameworthy for not acknowledging what they are; in other words, for being in bad faith. In a sense, then, the discussion will end where it begins—with Feuerbach's "irreligious criticism." But only in a sense. Along the way, much will be learned about why theism has survived into the modern era and about why its survival should be condemned. These findings will vindicate Feuerbach's contention that good faith is humanly possible. They will also underwrite the conviction, best articulated by Nietzsche but shared by the others, that the ultimate goal of irreligious criticism is to move civilization to a perspective beyond faith—to a form of life in which the opposition between faith and its antithesis is finally and definitively overcome. This was and to some extent still is one of the Left's main goals.

*   *   *

The claim that Abrahamic faith is bad faith is historically situated; it pertains only to those who do or ought to know better. Before enlightened thought penetrated the haze of Abrahamic civilization, that knowledge was harder to come by than it has since become. Thus, for most of the past two and a half millennia, the faith the Abrahamic religions promoted was not bad faith in the sense in question here. Bad faith is a modern development.

I will call the faith that preceded bad faith *full-blooded*, and I will suggest that, in some respects, bad faith is actually less onerous than its predecessor. Its emergence is a stage on a trajectory in which Abrahamic religiosity wanes as humanity advances towards the godless future Nietzsche and the others envisioned. Arguably, full-blooded faith survives only among the truly benighted, but there are alarmingly many believers nowadays whose faith at least appears to be full-blooded. It has become customary to call believers of this kind *fundamentalists*. I will not have much to say about this phenomenon, though I would question just how genuinely full-blooded faith can be in a world where news of what Nietzsche called the death of God has been in circulation for centuries. I would venture too that the fundamentalisms that currently wreak so much havoc around us have more to do with social and political than creedal factors, and that the faith of most fundamentalists is more like the bad faith of their contemporaries than may appear.

RATIONAL THEOLOGY

Why take the untenability of deism, and therefore of theism, for granted? The answer, in short, is that rational theology is a failed project. To be sure, those who seek to reconcile God and reason keep trying to breathe new life into the long-discredited arguments that comprise rational theology's core. Their efforts are sometimes ingenious, and it can be interesting and instructive to examine them. However, there is no need to do that here. To explain why Feuerbach, Durkheim, Nietzsche, and Freud assumed the irrationality of theistic convictions, it will suffice to focus on the broad contours of the case against rational theology.

First, though, we should recall what rational standards for belief acceptance are. To that end, it will be necessary to define some terms. From the days of Greek antiquity, it has been the received view that *rationality* has both practical and theoretical dimensions. *Practical reason* applies to actions and (social) practices; *theoretical reason* to beliefs. There is no firm agreement on what practical reason requires with respect to action; what a rational society is, is even more controversial. But the requirements of theoretical reason are universally accepted. Beliefs are rational if they can be defended by reasons of certain kinds; people are rational to the degree that they accept beliefs that are rationally defensible.

The gold standard has always been reasons of the kind set forth in logical demonstrations. Greek mathematics— geometry, in particular—provided the model: begin with compelling (ideally, self-evident) premises, elaborate their consequences through correct applications of truth-preserving rules of inference, and the consequences will be true in just the way that the premises are. Logical demonstrations of this kind are *deductive* arguments. Deductive arguments that rely upon correct applications of truth-preserving rules of inference are *valid*; valid arguments with true premises are *sound*. The conclusions of sound arguments are therefore true. It is irrational to deny conclusions that are established this way. Anyone who understands, for example, the proof of the Pythagorean theorem but denies its conclusion is *irrational*.

Needless to say, people are persuadable in any of a variety of non- or extralogical ways—including coercion, flattery, and outright chicanery presented in logical guise. Those of his contemporaries whom Socrates' followers, including Plato, called *sophists* were adept at the latter. Socrates insisted that sophistry was "base" and "ignoble," and that it was the enemy of true philosophy. His position still stands. For two and a half millennia, philosophers have insisted that, in principle, arguments should employ Socrates' standards, not the sophists', and that the most compelling arguments are those that emulate logical or mathematical demonstrations.

When people are not persuaded by sound deductive arguments, the problem may be that they do not understand them. When this is the case, it is often through no fault of their own. But even when they are culpable for not understanding, perhaps because they did not make enough of an effort, they are not irrational on this account. They are irrational only if they understand the argument and still reject its conclusion. Then they are at fault for being unmoved by the most "ennobling" kind of reason there is.

Sound deductive arguments have the force they do because they are *objective*. Objectivity contrasts with *subjectivity*. Reasons are subjectively compelling relative to particular persons or vantage points; objectively compelling reasons hold for everyone and from all possible vantage points. Because the argument establishing it is sound, the Pythagorean theorem is true for everyone everywhere. It may be that only we human beings can recognize its force. Were we the only rational beings in the universe, this would be the case. But even then it would not be because of anything intrinsically human that the argument compels assent; human beings *ought* to assent because they are rational. If there are rational beings who are not human, they too would be compelled to accept the Pythagorean theorem, provided, again, that they understand the argument that establishes it.

There is another rational standard, less powerful than the first, but with a broader range of application. The idea has also been in circulation for millennia, but it was not until the rise of the new physics in the seventeenth century that it became generally accepted and widely applied. According to this standard, beliefs are rational to the extent that evidence of an appropriate sort, empirical evidence, supports them. It is rational to accept such beliefs, albeit tentatively, awaiting new evidence or different ways of conceiving the issues in question or both, and it is similarly irrational to accept beliefs that are infirmed by pertinent evidence.

*　　*　　*

In the Christian tradition especially, but also in Islam and Judaism, there have been efforts to establish God's existence with arguments of a deductive character, based on purportedly unassailable (or already established) premises. These arguments consist of sentences that are either premises or that follow from preceding sentences by logical rules of inference, and they conclude with the sentence "God exists" or some ostensibly equivalent claim.

What rational theologians consider ostensibly equivalent

often bears only a very attenuated connection to "God exists." Therefore, questions can sometimes be raised about whether their arguments, if sound, would demonstrate that deism, much less theism, is true. The monumental *Summa Theologica* of Saint Thomas Aquinas (1225–1274) provides several examples. Aquinas purported to establish the existence of God in five ways.[3] Of these five, all but the last are deductive arguments.[4] The conclusions Aquinas reached are, respectively, that there is "a first mover, moved by no other"; that there is "a first efficient cause"; that there is a being "having of itself its own necessity, and not receiving it from another, but rather causing in others their necessity"; that there is "something which is to all beings, the cause of their being, goodness, and every other perfection"; and, finally, that "some intelligent being exists, by whom all natural things are directed to their end." In each case, having established these conclusions to his own satisfaction, Aquinas adds words to the effect that "this all men speak of as God." It is small wonder that the distinction drawn by Blaise Pascal (1623–1662) between "the God of the philosophers" and "the God of Abraham, Isaac, and Jacob" rings true.

However, questions about the relevance of the conclusions that purported demonstrations of God's existence reach are trivial in comparison to problems with the arguments themselves. Following a precedent established centuries ago, deductive arguments that aim to defend theism—or, rather, deism—are standardly categorized as *cosmological* or *ontological.* These names refer to argument types, not particular arguments. It is commonly said that arguments of the former type (the first four of the five arguments of Thomas Aquinas's are examples) appeal to "first causes." More strictly, they appeal implicitly to what has come to be called "the Principle of Sufficient Reason." According to that principle, for anything that exists or is the case, there is some reason why it is as it is and not otherwise. [5] Cosmological arguments begin by asserting some purportedly incontrovertible fact and then argue that this fact could not obtain unless, ultimately, God made it so; in other words, that God is the reason why it is as it is and not otherwise. In *The Critique of Pure Reason* (1781), Immanuel Kant argued persuasively that cosmological arguments misapply the principle they depend upon—that the Principle of Sufficient Reason rightly applies to everything that happens or is the case *within* experience, but not to experience itself. If he was right, as he almost certainly was, cosmological arguments are bound to fail no matter how cleverly constructed they may be.

Cosmological arguments have a certain intuitive plausibility inasmuch as we are inclined to look for causes, and because we are accustomed to think of God as an ultimate or fundamental cause. In contrast, ontological arguments seem patently sophistical. Whether or not this characterization is fair, it is plain that they are and always have been of more interest to philosophers concerned with such notions as "necessity" and "existence" than to believers. And difficult as ontological arguments may be to rebut, it is hard to imagine that anyone would be won over to faith on their account.

Unlike cosmological arguments, which depend on knowledge acquired from experience, ontological arguments depend on what we come to know by analyzing the concept "God." The inventor of this argument type, Saint Anselm (1033–1109) famously maintained that God "cannot be conceived so as not to exist." Because God is, by definition, a perfect being and because existence is an attribute of perfection, existence must be a property of God. Therefore, if we have a concept of God or, as Anselm put it, if "God exists in the understanding," "God exists in reality" too. Now God does exist in the understanding of anyone who asserts or denies his existence. Therefore, by the most venerable rule of logical inference, *Modus Ponens*, it follows that God exists.[6]

We can discover that, for example, tigers exist and that mermaids do not through empirical inquiry. If Anselm was right, we discover that God exists in another way altogether—the way we come to know that, for example, triangles have three sides or that bachelors are unmarried. We know that triangles are three-sided plane figures because we understand that any plane figure that is not three-sided would not count as a triangle. We know that bachelors are unmarried because we understand that what it is to be a bachelor is to be an unmarried man. But because existence is not a property of triangles or bachelors, triangles and bachelors can fail to exist, even if they cannot fail, if they do exist, to have three sides or to be unmarried. For defenders of cosmological arguments, it is different with God, and only with God. Because existence is one of his essential properties, whoever understands what God is must also come to know that he exists.

The mistake all ontological arguments make has been clear at least since Kant's devastating account of the main arguments of rational theology in *The Critique of Pure Reason*: ontological arguments misconstrue the nature of existence claims. Early twentieth-century developments in mathematical logic reinforce this criticism. In the view of logicians today, existence is not a *logical predicate*, as real properties are. It is a *logical operator*, a way of manipulating an assertion's truth-values without regard to the properties that its concepts designate. Ontological arguments treat existence as a predicate, not an operator. This is why they run aground.

An example taken (with modifications) from a venerable and still influential article written by the British philosopher G. E. Moore (1873–1958) illustrates this point in a perspicacious way.[7] Moore pointed out that the following sentences seem structurally equivalent in the sense that "growl" and "exist" are, in each case, grammatical predicates of the subject "tame tigers":

a) Tame tigers growl.
b) Tame tigers exist.

Thus it appears that (a) and (b) assert propositions of the same kind; that "growl" and "exist" both make assertions about what tame tigers do. But, in this instance (as in many others), grammar deceives us. "Growl" is a logical, as well as a grammatical, predicate; "exists" is a grammatical predicate only. Growling is therefore something tame tigers do; existing is not. This is why when "growl" is preceded by such words as "some" and "all," the classical operators of quantificational logic, what is asserted is distinct from what is asserted by (a);

while the same operation, applied to (b), produces very different results.

Thus:

c) *Some* tame tigers growl.

can be paraphrased to read "of all the tame tigers there are, there is at least one that growls." And:

(d) *All* tame tigers growl

can be paraphrased to read "all the tame tigers there are growl," or, equivalently, "there are no tame tigers that do not growl." But then the difference from "exist" is clear. The sentence

e) *Some* tame tigers exist

does not mean that, of the class of all tame tigers, at least one exists. It means that there are tame tigers. Similarly,

f) All tame tigers exist

does not mean that of all the tame tigers there are, none fail to exist. If this sentence makes a meaningful claim at all, it is the one made, more straightforwardly, by (e)—that there are tame tigers. In short, the grammatical similarity between "exists" and "growls" masks a logical difference.

Proponents of ontological arguments fail to realize this or, if they do, they fail to take its implications into account. They see no difference between existence, on the one hand, and omnipotence, omniscience, and perfect goodness, on the other. These are all purportedly attributes of perfection and therefore properties of a perfect being. But existence cannot be a property of a perfect being, "a being greater than which none can be conceived," because it is not a property at all. Grammar leads us to think otherwise, but it leads us astray.

Kant also identified a third sort of argument—the *teleological argument* or, as it is usually called today, *the argument from design*. Unlike cosmological and ontological arguments, arguments from design are not formal demonstrations; they do not purport to demonstrate that "God exists." They only aim to show that "God exists" is defensible according to the second rational standard for belief acceptance, evidential support. In this kind of argument, "God exists" is a hypothesis that the evidence of nature either sustains or disconfirms. Proponents of the argument maintain that a preponderance of evidence supports the hypothesis, and conclude, on this basis, that theism is rationally defensible.

The evidence is usually, though not necessarily, drawn from living organisms and systems. The contention is that the complexity observable in that evidence is of such a nature that it would be irrational to deny design and therefore irrational to deny that there is a designer. Kant was less critical of this argument type than of the others. But he did maintain, along with many others, that it makes an unwarranted inference based on a misleading analogy.[8] However, in the absence of a better explanation for the evidence in question, the design hypothesis arguably did once have some appeal. It could

36

always have been argued, even so, that chance accounts as well for the order we observe—a point acknowledged in David Hume's *Dialogues Concerning Natural Religion*.[9] But because appeals to chance are unintuitive, Hume was able to conclude his *Dialogues*, disingenuously but shrewdly, by declaring the argument from design correct. That was then; this is now. Two centuries ago it was still possible to hold that the best explanation for observable complexities in living organisms is an intelligent designer. It no longer is. Since Charles Darwin's discovery of evolution by natural selection almost a century and a half ago, a better, thoroughly naturalistic, explanation has been available. This is why the argument from design is no longer even remotely compelling. The argument defends the reasonableness of belief in God on the grounds that there is no better explanation for the evidence nature provides. But because there is a better explanation, the argument's conclusion must be rejected—for just the kind of reason its defenders deem apt.

Rational theology survives because believers refuse to let it go and because a few clever people persist in trying to defend the indefensible. However I have already said enough to justify what I, along with the authors I will discuss, assume—that, according to the standards for belief acceptance that we take for granted with respect to other existence claims, the idea that there exists an omnipotent, omniscient, perfectly good being does not begin to pass muster. If we add on the claims that this being created all that is and also somehow "relates" to human beings—in other words, if we invoke cosmological, ontological, or teleological arguments in support of theism, not just deism, the prospects for rational theology become even worse. We cannot prove definitively that God does *not* exist any more than we can prove that he does. But, insofar as rationality is the pertinent standard, there is no more reason to prove God's nonexistence in order to reject deism and therefore theism than there is to prove that Thor or Jupiter or, for that matter, Santa Claus do not exist in order to reject claims that they do.

*   *   *

Most of our beliefs about what is real are based on trust in what we are told by others; not on considerations we are able to provide for ourselves. There is nothing wrong with this so long as there is reason to be confident in those to whose authority or testimony we defer. This is why most of us believe, for example, that electrons exist. That belief is very likely true. But most people who think so cannot justify their position. Still, it is reasonable for them to believe that electrons exist because they suppose, correctly, that this contention *can* be justified; that *others,* qualified experts, are able to establish what they accept on authority. Because rational theology is a failed project, no one is justified in accepting theistic convictions on similar grounds.

It is widely assumed that, whether or not "God exists" is rationally defensible, there are non- or extrarational reasons to accept religious beliefs, and therefore to believe in God. This view is older than rational theology, and more pervasive. I will have more to say about non- or extrarational reasons for adopting a faith perspective in the pages that follow. For now, I would only note that all the Abrahamic religions maintain that what justifies at least some of their beliefs are *revelations*. This is one reason why the shortcomings of rational theology barely resonate even among thoughtful believers.

It is obvious, though, that revelation is useless for defending theism because it assumes what is in question. Only those who believe in God can plausibly accord authority to what he has revealed. God's revelations are problematic in any case, and not just because they are susceptible to differing, eminently contestable, interpretations. God is supposed to have made his will known in a remote and eerie past. His vague and equivocal words are remembered now because they were recorded years, sometimes centuries, later. For modern men and women to regard sources such as these, scriptural sources, as authoritative requires even more bad faith than believing in God Himself.

The testimony of persons who claim to have had direct access to the divine through mystical experiences raises different problems. I will not have much to say about mysticism here, except in connection with Freud's case for its cognitive irrelevance. It bears mention, though, that William James, a pioneer in the naturalistic study of religion, saw theism's best hope in just such testimony.[10] Perhaps he was right. But the grounds for hope are slight enough to be all but worthless.

CHAPTER ONE

ATHEISM
Young Hegelian Style

Following the death in 1833 of Germany's and the world's leading philosopher, Georg Wilhelm Friedrich Hegel, a handful of students and young professors in Berlin set out to advance the cause of revolution in Germany, extending Hegel's ideas by launching a "critique" of contemporaneous ("Right Hegelian") Protestant theology. These Young (or "Left") Hegelians included David Strauss, Bruno Bauer, Karl Neuwerck, Ludwig Feuerbach, Arnold Ruge, Max Stirner, Friedrich Engels, and Karl Marx; as remarkable a group of fledgling thinkers as ever joined together in a common project. Their rationale, the methods they deployed, and the substantive views they advanced seem exotic today, a relic of a long-ago moment in German thought.[1] Nevertheless, from roughly the 1950s through the 1980s, Marxists in Western countries took a keen interest in Young Hegelianism because they saw Marx's early, Young Hegelian writings as key to developing a "humanistic" version of Marxism. More recently, with interest in Marxism on the wane, interest in Young Hegelianism has subsided. This is unfortunate because what we can still learn from Feuerbach and the others is more timely than ever.

I will not dwell on the movement's history or internal divisions, but to understand its contemporary relevance, it is necessary to say something about Young Hegelianism in its own time and place. Following Marx's lead, I will assume that Feuerbach's *The Essence of Christianity* was, at once, the movement's seminal work and crowning achievement.[2] Because Feuerbach influenced Marx, and because Young Hegelianism is inevitably viewed through a Marxist prism, this is a standard position. But even if Feuerbach's place in the Young Hegelian movement was less central than it seems to those who are mainly interested in Marx, the fact remains that his masterwork is immensely instructive for anyone interested in Abrahamic religiosity. To contemporary readers, *The Essence of Christianity* can seem a strange collation. This is hardly surprising: it is an intervention into philosophical and political debates that faded into obscurity long ago, and its underlying metaphysics is problematic at best. However, this is a rare instance in which God is *not* in the details. Feuerbach's larger themes matter more than his particular contentions or his efforts to defend them.

*   *   *

In *The Essence of Christianity*, Feuerbach had two interconnected aims: to develop a "philosophical anthropology," or, what comes to the same thing, an account of the human essence; and to explain theism in anthropological terms—revealing the human (anthropological) meaning that belief in God simultaneously expresses and conceals. Feuerbach also sought to uncover the human meanings of concepts that cluster around the God idea for which the concept of God is foundational. *Criticism* is the methodology Feuerbach devised for these purposes. It is a hermeneutical or interpretive method; a translation program, so to speak, that aims at what would nowadays be called a "theoretical reduction"—where one theory is recast in terms of another, more fundamental theory. In *The Essence of Christianity*, Feuerbach's aim was to translate Right Hegelian Protestant theology, which he regarded as the most developed account of religious experience, into Young (Left) Hegelian philosophical anthropology, a theory he considered fundamental for reasons I will discuss. However, unlike an ordinary translation, criticism does not just identify equivalences. It eliminates the theory that is reduced away—in this case, the theology. Feuerbach seems to have thought that reducing a theory away dispatches what the theory represents; that it eliminates the theory's "object" along with its representation. It is not clear how this could be true generally or even what it would mean in most instances; but, as we will see, for Protestant theology as Feuerbach conceived it, his position does make sense.

Feuerbach had no need to rebut Christianity's foundational claim that "God exists"; that task was only preliminary to what he had in mind and it had been accomplished decades earlier. Indeed, there is a sense in which the critical program he devised establishes Christianity's truth—not literally, of course, but by showing that, in being false in the way it is, it expresses truths about humankind. Christianity misrepresents the truths it expresses, and its misrepresentations keep humanity in thrall. Feuerbach thought that reducing the theology of his Right Hegelian contemporaries to a true philosophical anthropology would emancipate humankind from Christianity's sway. Thus he took up earlier efforts to throw off Christianity's yoke not by showing, yet again, that theism (or deism) is indefensible, but by uncovering the human meanings that the God idea and all that rests upon it simultaneously express and conceal.

*   *   *

By their own lights, Feuerbach and the others were embarked on an emancipatory project that brings philosophy's history, as they conceived it, to an end—melding it into revolutionary politics.

The Young Hegelians developed their account of their role in German philosophy and politics by drawing on Hegel's *Phenomenology of Mind* [*Geist*], published in 1807, and from the material published posthumously in his *Lectures on the Philosophy of History* and in his *Lectures on The History of Philosophy.* A certain conception of philosophy emerges from their reflections on these texts—one that emphasizes, and arguably exaggerates, Hegel's importance, and therefore the importance of his followers, including themselves. But however questionable their account of philosophy's trajectory may be, their conception of what philosophers do, shorn of its Hegelian entanglements, is sound and widely shared. For Feuerbach and the other Young Hegelians, philosophy is not so much about doctrines as about resolving puzzlements of a broadly conceptual nature. To this end, philosophers construct theories, accounts guided by rational standards, of general and abstract notions—such as goodness and beauty and the nature of the real. Of course, these theories can be construed as doctrines. But not all collections of doctrines count as philosophies. Bodies of doctrine exist nearly everywhere and at all times. However, philosophy's way of making sense of the world, its distinctive project, has a determinate history; a beginning, a middle, and an end—or rather two epochal beginnings, middles, and ends.

Its first phase began in ancient Greece and developed, over two thousand years, in fits and starts until it was begun again, definitively and for the final time, in seventeenth-century Europe. This last new beginning is epitomized in the work of a several magisterial philosophers, of whom René Descartes (1596–1650) was the most influential. What Descartes and the others inaugurated culminated late in the eighteenth century in the work of Immanuel Kant. Hegel and his followers did not claim that Kant "solved" all the problems that philosophers had posed since Greek antiquity. Their idea, instead, was that, after the great seventeenth-century philosophers reconceived philosophy, the forms and limits of knowledge became its principal concern, and efforts to defend or combat skepticism became its central focus. In their view, Kant finally defeated skepticism by showing how knowledge of "the external world" is possible. In doing so, he also made clear what the entire philosophical project, from its beginnings to his own day, had been about. It was about Freedom, an idea that worked its way to full self-consciousness through the unfolding of philosophical representations of humanity's real history.

This discovery set the stage for philosophy's second and final epochal phase. Kant had distinguished the *actual* world human beings experience, a *phenomenal* order that exists in space and time and that is governed by the principle of causality, from the *real* or *noumenal* order of things-in-themselves, the abode of the idea of freedom. He held that while we can establish that things-in-themselves, noumenal things, are real, knowledge of them must remain forever beyond our grasp. This separation of the actual from the real, where the former is cognitively accessible and the latter is not, gave rise to a new set of problems, the resolution of which became the task of "classical German philosophy." In order to join the actual and the real in the way he ultimately did, it fell to Hegel to represent the structure of reality itself. He did so by identifying the real with the rational; in other words, with reason itself. This line of thinking led Hegel to maintain that reality is dialectical in the sense that its constituent subjects and objects interact with and thereby transform one another continuously. For as long as the dialectic unfolds, the real is in a process of *becoming*—in which, on Hegel's account, what is, an *affirmation* or *thesis*, develops its own *negation* or *antithesis* with which it is in internal opposition or *contradiction*, until its contradictory "moments" are incorporated into a higher unity, a *synthesis* or *supersession* (*Aufhebung*).

Hegel held that the idea of freedom—the core notion of Kant's practical (as distinct from his theoretical) philosophy and, for that reason, of his purchase on the noumenal order—is an essentially historical notion. Following his lead, all of Hegel's followers, Right and Left, agreed that, ultimately, freedom can and must be realized in actual history. Both sides also agreed that this "end" or culmination of classical German philosophy is attained when Freedom is embodied institutionally in a state organized around principles of universal Right (*Recht*), a *Rechtstaat*. Their quarrel was therefore not so much philosophical as political. For the Right Hegelians, Prussia, their homeland, was already a *Rechtstaat*. The Right Hegelians were therefore defenders of the status quo. For the Young (Left) Hegelians, the Prussian state was the penultimate, not the final, "moment" in freedom's story; and the only way forward was to transform it completely—to revolutionize it.

Thus the Young Hegelians had a fundamental political disagreement with their Right Hegelian rivals. But the arguments they advanced were philosophical, not political. As Hegelians, they maintained that as the idea of freedom unfolds towards its "end" (*telos*), the actual becomes the "inversion" of the real. This was how they conceived the Prussian state; so far from implementing freedom it was a realm in which unfreedom reached its maximum extent. Thus the urgency of setting inverted institutions on their feet—emancipating humankind by bringing the actual into line with the real. For Feuerbach and the others, what began in ancient Greece and ended with Hegel's completion of the work of classical German philosophy therefore culminates in revolutionary politics.

*　　*　　*

The Young Hegelians faulted the Right Hegelians because, like Hegel, they were *idealists*, not *materialists*. Correcting that mistake was another task the Young Hegelians took upon themselves.

As noted, when Descartes and the others relaunched the first epochal stage of the philosophical project, they put the question "What can I know?" in the foreground. From its beginnings, *ontology*, the theory of what is, had been a central philosophical concern. Descartes subordinated ontology to *epistemology*, the theory of knowledge; for him, what is, is just what we can know to be. Other leading philosophers concurred. With this conviction in place, Descartes went on to show, to his own satisfaction and to the satisfaction of many others, that there are two kinds of things we can know to be, two *substances*: ideal substance, Mind; and material substance, Matter. The former is mental—thinking is its essence—and nonspatial; the latter is spatial—extension is its essence—and mind-independent. When Descartes invoked the category of substance, he had in mind roughly what his predecessors in the "scholastic" tradition did. This is why he insisted that substances are radically independent of one another in the sense that the conditions in virtue of which they are what they are in no way depend on their relations with other substances. This raised a vexing question: How can Mind and Matter, the substances Descartes identified, causally interact? How can material events have mental consequences and vice versa? These interactions occur in each and every one of us all the time. But, if Mind and Matter are radically independent, how is this possible?

Descartes proposed a patently unsatisfactory solution to this problem—that mind and matter connect in the pineal gland through the medium of "animal spirits." Philosophers who agreed with him on the substantial nature of what *is* did no better. This was a major reason why it soon became the dominant view in ontology that there must ultimately be only one substance; why *Cartesian dualism,* the idea that there are two and only two substances, mind and matter, gave way to one or another version of *monism,* the idea that everything that is, is of the same substantial nature. Thanks to Descartes's continuing influence, the substances he identified were the contenders—even for those who rejected his epistemological positions along with his dualism. Thus the two monisms that emerged as "modern" (post-Cartesian) philosophy unfolded were descendants of Cartesian dualism. Monists who maintained that everything that is, including ostensibly material things like physical objects, are ultimately mental in nature were *idealists*; monists who maintained that everything, including ostensibly mental things like pains or sensations, are ultimately material were *materialists.*

Kant and Hegel were idealists, as were most of their more distinguished predecessors, but there were materialist philosophers too. Some of them took it upon themselves to refute deism (theism). Thus materialism came to be identified with atheism in philosophical circles. And because these materialists sought the overthrow of political and clerical elites who championed theism and used it to control the masses of people they dominated, materialism also came to be associated with revolutionary politics. Conversely, idealism was associated with theism and conservative politics. There were exceptions, of course, but the idea that metaphysical, theological, and political positions were connected in these ways—not just for contingent historical reasons, but for conceptual reasons too—was a tenet of the intellectual culture the Young Hegelians inherited. It had been so for decades and it would remain so throughout the nineteenth century and, thanks to Communism, into the twentieth century as well.

Feuerbach endorsed Hegel's dialectical method but, unlike Hegel, he was a materialist—and an atheist and revolutionary. Hegel would probably have deemed Feuerbach's configuration of methodological and ontological positions incoherent. The Right Hegelians certainly thought so, and they may have been right. But even if a genuinely dialectical materialism is possible, it is far from obvious that Feuerbach succeeded in confecting one.[3] It is telling that, after he broke away from Feuerbach's ambit, Marx insisted that he had not.[4]

Feuerbach differed from Hegel on another key issue. Hegel's philosophy was about abstract, historical processes, not the career of man or any other historically developing "subject."[5] In contrast, Feuerbach's philosophy was a "philosophical anthropology," a theory of the human subject. However, Feuerbach was Hegelian enough not to be a naturalist. His philosophical anthropology took no account of universal psychological properties or anything else susceptible to empirical investigation; it was metaphysical and *essentialist* instead. Feuerbach thought that the way to account for what human beings are is to identify essential metaphysical (non- or extranatural) properties that define the human subject; and that doing so is indispensable for ending the project that began after Kant concluded the first epochal stage of philosophy's history. In his view, the questions posed within classical German philosophy, philosophy's final epochal phase, are rightly recast as questions *about* the human meaning of everything that is in all its apparently heterogeneous forms as human history, moving inexorably towards its end (*telos*), unfolds.

The idea that there is a human essence—that there are *essential*, not just *accidental* properties all human beings share—is itself a metaphysical contention. It was in this vein that Aristotle famously maintained that man is a rational animal, that rationality is an essential human trait and that no other property, except being an animal, is. Being shorter than ten feet tall would therefore not be essential for being human even if, as a matter of fact, no human being has ever exceeded ten feet in height and none ever will. Being shorter than ten feet is an accidental, not an essential, property of being human inasmuch as a rational animal taller than ten feet, if one existed, would, in Aristotle's view, still count as human. On the other hand, an animal without rationality could never count as human. An *essence* is a set of conditions necessary and sufficient for being what one is. Aristotle's claim that man is a rational animal is a claim about the human essence, about necessary and sufficient conditions for being human.

Feuerbach's metaphysical essentialism is of a piece with this contention. Thus his claim that there is a human essence was hardly original. What was original was his account of what the human essence is. Also original, and non-Aristotelian, was his insistence that because it renders human meanings accessible to consciousness, a true and complete philosophical anthropology, a theory of essential humanity, is key to realizing the ultimate goal of the philosophical project. There is, however, a distinguished precedent even for this contention; Kant anticipated it. In *The Critique of Pure Reason*, Kant wrote that "What can I know?" "What ought I to do?" and "What can I hope?" are the fundamental philosophical questions.[6] In a later work, *Anthropology from a Pragmatic Point of View* (1798), he went on to suggest that, in the final analysis, these three questions reduce to one: "What is man?" However, Kant never defended this arguably hyperbolic assertion, nor did he work out its implications. These too were tasks that Feuerbach and the other Young Hegelians took upon themselves.

Notwithstanding their identification with Hegel, the Young Hegelian reduction program was fundamentally Kantian. Feuerbachian "criticism" was methodologically innovative, but it was still criticism in the sense of Kant's three *Critiques*.[7] Kantian criticism aimed to establish "the conditions for the possibility" of one or another form of experience. As philosophical anthropologists, the Young Hegelians maintained that it is ultimately essential humanity that makes the heterogeneous ways that experience presents itself possible. Their aim in doing philosophy—or rather, criticism—was to draw out the consequences of this purported truth by laying bare the human meanings experience expresses.

Thus Feuerbach's philosophical anthropology was, in effect, a general theory of everything; an account of what everything *means*. That meaning is always and everywhere the same because, in the end, everything has a *human* meaning. And if everything means the same thing, everything must ultimately be the same thing. Feuerbach took this conclusion to follow from his materialist ontology. This is not as odd as may appear. For all monists, whether they be materialists or idealists, at the deepest metaphysical level, there is only one real thing. For Hegel, the one real thing was spirit (*Geist*) becoming conscious of itself; for the Young Hegelians, it was man becoming what he essentially is. In both cases, essential unity is recovered through a process of *becoming*. Philosophy's and then criticism's goal is to comprehend this process and to carry it forward.

To execute the critical program, to reduce Right Hegelian theology to philosophical anthropology, it is necessary, of course, that the philosophical anthropology be available. *The Essence of Christianity* was Young Hegelianism's seminal work because it constructed that anthropology.

Because everything ultimately means the same thing, criticism of any aspect of human experience leads in principle to the same result. The essence of Christianity is the human essence, and the human essence is the essence of everything else as well. Nevertheless, the critical program could not have begun anywhere other than where it did; as Marx put it, "the criticism of religion is the premise of all criticism."[8] This is so because the God idea, which all Hegelians agreed finds its most developed expression in Protestant theology, designates an "object" that is entirely immaterial and therefore utterly unreal. God is *nothing but* a representation in inverted (or "alienated") form of essential humanity. Ironically, God's immateriality—and therefore his nonexistence—enabled Feuerbach to develop a philosophical anthropology. The truth about man is no more inherent in religious experience than in anything else, but everywhere else human meanings are embodied in real (material) things and are therefore less transparent. Insofar as the task is to develop a philosophical anthropology and not just to use it in a reduction program, transparency is indispensable; hence the need to start where Feuerbach did. Only when man objectifies his essence in an object that is utterly without substance, in God, is the objectification perspicacious enough to serve Feuerbach's purpose.

This is why criticism of a definitive articulation of the God idea is the key to the general theory. After it is complete, humanity will finally have arrived at full self-awareness; it will know the truth about itself. The critical program can then be applied to other aspects of human experience—specifically, to matters of more direct concern to revolutionaries.[9] And after criticism of representations of other pertinent forms of experience has run its course, there will be nothing left but for "the arm of criticism" to pass into "the criticism of arms," as Marx famously proclaimed."[10] A social and political revolution will follow, propelling man into the realm of freedom—the "end" idealist philosophy discovered but could never in principle attain.

* * *

Thus the Young Hegelians were motivated by theoretical exigencies immanent in classical German philosophy, but also by political concerns. These motivations combined to give rise to a way of thinking that produced an atheism of an unprecedented kind.

By their own account, Feuerbach and the others comprised a philosophical and political vanguard ensconced in a country populated by a people in the thrall of theistic beliefs and the ecclesiastical institutions that sustained them. Like the materialist philosophers of pre–Revolutionary France with whom they identified, they were anticlerical and antitheist. But their attitude towards the theism of their compatriots was not dismissive in the manner of those philosophers. Neither were they German versions of the "village atheists" of American lore. Unlike those atheists and their counterparts today, Young Hegelian atheism was cognizant of the ways theism addresses the deepest human concerns at the same time that it was hostile to theism and determined to free humanity from its harms.

Like his Right Hegelian rivals, Feuerbach made much of Christianity's affective side. As a creature of the Romantic age and of a Protestant culture, he was disposed to favor inwardness, enchantment, reverence, and awe. He and his cothinkers therefore had little sympathy for the heartless, mechanistic worldview of earlier generations. But Feuerbach was as much opposed to faith in the God of Abraham, Isaac, and Jacob as any of his predecessors. Unlike them, however, he did not just want to reject the faith he opposed; he wanted to incorporate it, in Hegelian fashion, into a "higher unity" along with its antithesis. Thus he aimed to establish a faith in which God has no role, but in which man, essential humanity, did. Feuerbach thought that Christianity pointed the way towards a faith partisans of progress could endorse. It does so because the essence of Christianity is the human essence; because, in the final analysis, Christianity is not about God, but about man.

Feuerbach thought too that becoming aware of the truths theism conceals, not just cognitively but also affectively, is personally and politically emancipatory. He and the other Young Hegelians were confident of the political, indeed revolutionary, efficacy of the fundamental reorientation of consciousness criticism produced. They were convinced that coming to terms with the fact that man makes God, not vice versa, is enough to transform former believers into agents of revolutionary change.[11]

* * *

Although all Young Hegelians acknowledged the need to launch the critical program where Feuerbach did, most of them were not interested in religion as such. Marx was hardly typical in this respect or any other, but his example is illustrative; he always had more important things to think about than a deity who doesn't exist. In his midtwenties, Marx broke with Young Hegelianism altogether; as he declared in the long section on Feuerbach in *The German Ideology*, written in 1845 but published posthumously, he "settled accounts with his erstwhile philosophical conscience." But even while he was still Feuerbach's disciple, he wrote almost nothing about religion per se. When he was no longer a Young Hegelian, he wrote even less.

Nevertheless, what he did write while a Young Hegelian is widely known and misunderstood: religion, Marx declared, is "the opium of the people." According to the usual understanding, these words suggest that Marx thought that faith was nothing more than a means cynical ruling classes use to narcotize the populations they rule into submission. He did think ruling classes use religion this way, and no doubt they do. But Marx's words convey a different thought as well, a distinctively Feuerbachian insight. Thus his claim that religion is the opium of the people was preceded by this:

> Religious suffering is at once the *expression* of real suffering and the *protest* against real suffering. Religion is the sigh of the oppressed creature, the heart of a heartless world, just as it is the spirit of spiritless conditions....[12]

Marx wrote these words at the beginning of a reflection on Young Hegelianism's role in the years immediately ahead, years that would precede revolutionary upheavals. To this end, he felt obliged to say something about Young Hegelianism's past. But he had no interest in revisiting Feuerbach's account of Christianity, and neither did he think it necessary to improve upon Feuerbach's philosophical anthropology. In his view, Feuerbach had gotten Christianity and philosophical anthropology right. It was time to move on to the next order of business and, ultimately, to revolutionary politics itself.

After breaking with Feuerbach, Marx turned away from the critical program altogether. Instead of applying Feuerbachian criticism to ethics and politics or to the emerging science of political economy, he forged new ways of making sense of the "the laws of motion" of capitalist societies and of world history generally. This was a momentous change of focus, undertaken, in part, because he had come to the conclusion that irreligious criticism and its extensions into other areas of human experience was no longer as politically consequential as it had been, or had seemed to be; and in part because his philosophical orientation had changed. Other Young Hegelians went their own ways as well. The "moment" of Feuerbachian criticism passed.

What ended was a stage in the history of atheism that contemporary atheists foolishly ignore. That it came into being at all is remarkable. Right Hegelianism was a bulwark upon which defenders of the status quo staked their case, a "discourse" of oppression. How tempting it must therefore have been to disparage the beliefs it defended, and to leave the matter at that! But the Young Hegelians resisted this temptation, seeking instead to retrieve what is of human value in a faith that is deleterious to human wellbeing. That would be the way it does service as the "opium of the people"; the way it speaks to fundamental human needs, even as it misrepresents those needs and impedes human emancipation.

However, the Young Hegelians did succumb to a different temptation. As Marx would describe with consummate sarcasm in *The German Ideology*, they exaggerated the importance of their own endeavors. For it was their view that a German revolution would become inevitable once irreligious criticism took hold of the consciousness of believers in Germany. This was an extreme version of a common conceit. Nevertheless, it seemed plain to the Young Hegelians, as it then still did to enlightened and radical thinkers elsewhere, that it is only necessary to spread the word for theistic faith, bad faith, to disappear. Well into the twentieth century, this remained a widespread view. Many liberals believed it. Socialists and anarchists did too. They realized that the way forward would be neither easy nor direct. Elites would continue to use religion to control subaltern layers of social hierarchies, and clerisies would not relinquish their wealth and power without a struggle. But, in the end, light would triumph over darkness. Within a few generations at most, religion would become a historical memory, a relic of an unenlightened past.

This was and still is a reasonable expectation for those who believe in the power of reason to sway the human mind. However, belief in theism's imminent demise has become increasingly difficult to sustain. The religions enlightened thinkers inveighed against more than two centuries ago should no longer matter politically; they should no longer even exist. But they do exist and they do matter. Indeed, they seem to matter more than ever. Thus we are today, again, in a situation which, in at least one important respect, is similar to the one the Young Hegelians encountered—religion is, more than usually, an obstacle in the way of human progress. Accordingly, a Young Hegelian response, shorn of the obscurantist metaphysics and the undue optimism of the original version, is called for again. A determined but nondismissive atheism, intent on incorporating what good faith can retrieve from bad, will not by itself set the world aright, but it can help enormously in moving humanity closer to that end.

Because they believed that a social and political revolution was imminent, the Young Hegelians had no time for that "pessimism of the intellect" that Antonio Gramsci recommended along with "optimism of the will."[13] They therefore had nothing to say about the future of Christianity except that it would lose its reason for being; and they had nothing to say about how the Left should deal with Christians or adherents of other Abrahamic faiths in years to come. Why should they? They were sure that the Abrahamic religions have no future except for a while in benighted quarters; that, in short order, addictions to the "opium of the people" would expire along with the world's *anciens régimes*. They soon discovered that their expectations were wrong on all counts. However they were not wrong in thinking that "taking consciousness"—facing reality—is a condition for changing life for the better. Their error was to inflate this facet of a larger emancipatory project into a full-fledged, stand-alone strategic program.

*   *   *

One way to deal with believers, when enlightenment fails, is to repress belief. "Militant atheism" was the norm in Communist countries, where the coercive power of the state was deployed to discourage and sometimes proscribe faith perspectives. Realizing that this was a lost cause, at least in the short run, the Communists were seldom thoroughgoing in their efforts to excise faith; but, in fits and starts, they tried. Marxists out of power could only persuade believers to come to their senses; they could hardly force them. In time, though, Marxists, including Communists, sought to make common cause with believers—especially in countries where there were strong, reform-minded Catholic political parties. Thus, by the middle of the twentieth century, the positions on religion advanced by most Marxists in non-Communist countries verged on liberalism. This is not the only respect in which Marxist and liberal positions increasingly converged. But it is an especially telling one inasmuch as the histories of liberalism and of religious toleration are intertwined. Even so, it bears mention that, in the past, many liberals agreed with the goals militant atheists advanced. Their quarrel was with their means; they considered them inadmissible or ineffective or both.

The Young Hegelians discussed religious toleration only in the course of faulting philosophical and political orientations that they deemed insufficiently radical because they envisioned nothing beyond liberal horizons. They saw no need to incorporate liberal practices into their political program because they were sure that making the human meaning of theistic concepts known would vanquish religion altogether. This is why they had nothing to say about believers who resist their explanations. But had the movement survived long enough for Young Hegelians to have had no choice but to confront the issue, they would probably not have opposed militant atheism on strictly liberal grounds, but because politically organized efforts to suppress faith are at odds with the spirit of Young Hegelian criticism. What they thought Feuerbach had contrived was an explanatory program that would result in people freeing themselves from theistic ideas and the institutions associated with them. Theirs was a project of mass self-emancipation that took no explicit notice of inviolable individual rights, while nevertheless protecting individuals' lives and behaviors from illiberal interferences.

As Communism's experience with militant atheism suggests, the battle *against* theism, much less *for* Young Hegelian atheism, cannot be waged successfully at the level of institutions, policies, and laws alone. And, as Feuerbach and the other Young Hegelians well knew, having better arguments will not suffice either. There is no alternative to a protracted cultural struggle; one that takes into account all the factors that have made religion, from time immemorial, a palliative for the suffering of the oppressed, an opium of the people. Only a war waged in and over the ambient intellectual culture can, in time, render the Abrahamic religions as politically inert as, say, the wiser, but similarly unsustainable polytheisms they replaced.[14]

* * *

The Young Hegelians maintained that the only good faith is atheistic, and they saw "irreligious criticism," their means for establishing good faith, as a decisive step in the struggle to realize the Left's aspirations in the conditions of their time and place. We now know that they profoundly underestimated the difficulties in the way of weaning man, the creator, off God, his creation, just as we now know how wrong they were to think that doing so by itself would give rise to a social and political revolution that would establish heaven—or rather a form of life that captures what is possible in Christianity's inverted idea of heaven—on earth. But the Young Hegelians were right to insist that it is not enough to win every (intellectual) battle, and that even false beliefs express basic truths that partisans of progress must cognitively and affectively embrace if they are to change themselves and the world. They were right, too, to insist that irreligious criticism can be politically consequential, even as they disabled themselves politically by overestimating its importance. These facets of the Young Hegelian program remain timely; if anything, the passage of time has made them even more urgent than they were in Feuerbach's day. This is why, along with more momentous forms of struggle, the battles Feuerbach and the other Young Hegelians waged in historically particular and philosophically dubious ways must be fought and (re)won, however many times it takes, until humanity moves on—definitively and irreversibly.

CHAPTER TWO

A SOCIAL THING

Feuerbach thought that all aspects of experience ultimately have a human meaning, and that human beings express essential humanity in all that they do. He thought that theism represents this fact of the human condition with unparalleled clarity and that demonstrating that this is so, revealing the human meaning that theistic ideas express and conceal, was an urgent task for revolutionaries in his time and place. Because they believed that a revolution was imminent, and because they harbored no doubts about its success, Feuerbach and the others had nothing to say about God's fate in a world where enlightenment does not prevail. They also overestimated the prospects for revolutionary change in their immediate future, and they never looked beyond this short-term horizon.

This is not the only respect in which Feuerbach and the others were myopic. They focused on meanings but, because they were only concerned with matters directly pertinent to the revolution to come, their view of what human beings do to organize their lives in meaningful ways was, at best, parochial and their findings were narrower than need be. This is why they never quite grasped how the quest for meaning inherent in human nature is a condition for the possibility of any and all social cohesion; in other words, how religion is a social thing.

For that insight to register, it will be instructive to turn to Émile Durkheim's account of religion's beginnings in *The Elementary Forms of Religious Life* (1912). Durkheim and Feuerbach stand poles apart. Nevertheless, their positions on faith are complementary in ways that support the contention that adherents of Abrahamic religions in postenlightened times exhibit bad faith.

*   *   *

Feuerbach and the other Young Hegelians maintained that theism is false but true *in a sense* because it *expresses* in a distorted, indeed "inverted," way true claims about the human essence. I would venture that many, perhaps most, self-identified believers in the modern period also think that their beliefs are true only in some nonliteral sense. If so, they prevaricate in a way the Young Hegelians did not. To be sure, the Young Hegelians were empathic atheists, but they were atheists above all. Those who hold theistic convictions while agreeing with Feuerbach and the others on the literal falseness of the beliefs they profess are in bad faith. So far from confronting reality squarely, they turn away from it—denying, perhaps to themselves but certainly to others, what their faith is about.

This realization brings us back to the puzzlement Feuerbach and Durkheim—and also Freud and Nietzsche—addressed: If theism is false, as it plainly is, and if it is widely understood to be false, why do so many cling to it? One reason why we do not have a good answer is that the issue is seldom addressed. The reasons for this are, in part, historical. Throughout history, clerical and political authorities, acting in concert in those instances where they were not one and the same, established order by enforcing orthodoxy—targeting not only illiterate subjects, but educated elites as well. Their efforts were largely successful; in most times and places, it was extremely difficult to examine theological convictions critically. In Christian countries it was especially difficult inasmuch as Christianity's ascendancy in the West, and to a lesser extent also in the Byzantine East, coincided with a decline in learning that persisted for nearly a millennium. Of course, there were heretics and schismatics, and remnants of paganism also survived. But theism itself was never significantly challenged. Perhaps atheists existed. But they were invisible or mired in impenetrable layers of self-deception or both. Belief in God was no more tenable then than it is today. But this fact fell beyond the ken of nearly everyone's awareness.

This is no longer the case, especially in liberal societies where heterodox opinions are tolerated and sometimes even encouraged. But the question is pertinent wherever glimmers of enlightenment penetrate, whether or not religious freedom is assured. Even so, adequate and comprehensive explanations for theism's tenacity are wanting—in part because the issues involved are complex, but also because the problem is still only rarely addressed, even as the old forms of social control have waned. Ironically, liberalism itself is partly to blame. In sequestering religion into a private sphere of individual conscience, it has sheltered it from public criticism—creating a "space" for bad faith to thrive. Lately, liberals have made a virtue of this failing. No doubt, some of them are believers but even those who are not have been loath to depict the religiosity of others as a problem calling for an explanation on the grounds that it would be uncivil to suggest that the beliefs of their fellow citizens merit condemnation. Overweening civility in the public arena has even become a matter of principle in influential liberal circles.[1] Robert Frost is supposed to have said that a liberal is someone who won't take his own side in an argument. As a generalization, this may be too harsh. But where faith is concerned, it is an apt observation.

Durkheim was a liberal, but he was not shy about subjecting religious beliefs and practices to critical scrutiny. He was also a founder of modern sociology. It is therefore not surprising that his account of religion was sociological. This observation bears notice because, in assessing matters of faith, a sociological perspective can seem counterintuitive. It is natural to look to psychology, not sociology, for an explanation for theism's hold over the human mind. This is especially the case in liberal societies. With faith relegated to a private sphere, officially immune from state *and* societal interference, it would seem that theism's preternatural resistance to extinction must depend only on individuals' dispositions towards religiosity. This was William James's view in his monumental account of the psychology of the faithful (and faithless), *The Varieties of Religious Experience.*[2] It was also the view of Sigmund Freud. An implication of this line of thinking is that the God that theologians and religious philosophers try in vain to defend and the spontaneous theism to which human beings are susceptible are, at best, in tension because theism's appeal has little to do with rational standards for belief acceptance; it depends instead on non- or extrarational psychological causes. This is one reason why rational theology's failures have done less damage to faith perspectives than enlightened thinkers anticipated. Rebuttals that rely on reason alone are of little consequence against beliefs we are psychologically disposed to accept.

The Young Hegelians were proponents of a faith that is honest, rationally defensible, and as "moving" as the faith they sought to vanquish. They wanted to "negate" Christianity; a crucial, perhaps even an indispensable, step in overcoming (superseding) it altogether. But for the kind of faith Feuerbach envisioned to be humanly possible, elements of the faith he sought to negate must be able to survive Christianity's (and Judaism's and Islam's) demise. Although his topic was "primitive" religion, some of the claims Durkheim advanced in *The Elementary Forms of Religious Life* bear on this prospect. *The Elementary Forms* is about theism's past, not its present or future. Nevertheless, Durkheim's account of religion yields insights into the nature and durability of "nonelementary" forms of religious life as well.

One of Durkheim's unstated but barely hidden objectives in *The Elementary Forms,* as in many other writings of his, was to defend *social,* as distinct from psychological, explanations of social facts; and, more specifically, to develop functionalist and structuralist explanatory strategies for the social sciences. His insistence on the autonomy of sociology is no longer controversial. His functionalism and structuralism have not fared as well. It is not necessary, though, to accept Durkheim's general theoretical orientation to learn a great deal about bad faith and good and about the prospects for overcoming faith altogether from *The Elementary Forms of Religious Life*. What follows is therefore selective and also, for the most part, agnostic about the merits of Durkheim's general theoretical framework. Neither will I question the soundness of the evidence he presented. Durkheim drew on the best ethnographic data of his time. A century later, more is known, and understandings have evolved. But this is another instance where God is *not* in the details. Durkheim's insights into religion's role in human life are more apparent in the broad contours of the story he tells than in its twists and turns.

*   *   *

Like all Hegelians, Feuerbach and his cothinkers were holists; they thought that to make sense of anything in particular, it is necessary to understand its relations with other components of the "whole" or "totality" of which it is a part.[3] The Young Hegelians therefore resisted the Aristotelian idea, assumed throughout modern science, that reality is comprised of discrete "natural kinds," each of which can be explained without reference to other natural kinds or to the totality they comprise. Hegelians were not hostile to science. But they agreed with Kant that it can only yield knowledge of what is empirically accessible, and therefore that things-in-themselves lie beyond its scope. But they did not conclude, as Kant did, that reality is unknowable. They thought that Hegel had shown how we can apprehend things-in-themselves by deploying extrascientific, dialectical ways of knowing. In their view, the "dialectical logic" Hegel developed tracks the real movement of the whole—which realizes itself through the development of "contradictions" that are continually "superseded" by ever more developed expressions of the real until the reality that underlies everything, the reality that all appearances express, realizes all the potentialities inherent in it.

As remarked, the Young Hegelians were materialists, not idealists like Hegel or their Right Hegelian rivals. However, to be a materialist and also a dialectician, ontology and methodology must be independent of one another to the extent that Hegel's account of the substantial nature of what is, his idealist ontology, can be "stood on its feet," as the saying goes, while his methodology remains unchanged. The idea that form and content can be dissociated this way is, on the face of it, implausible and un-Hegelian. But Feuerbach and the others were adamant: they believed that the method Hegel contrived for representing the Mind's path to self-awareness is integral to a materialist, not an idealist, ontology, and therefore that it is Matter, not Mind, that has a dialectical structure.

On this basis, they imported core Hegelian doctrines into the critical program—among them, the idea that there is ultimately no distinction between values and facts. For nondialecticians, the two are logically independent; it is one thing to explain what is the case and something else to assert what ought to be. But, within a dialectical framework, the way things *really* are is the way they ought to be. There is therefore an imperative to move the process along: to encourage the actual to become what it really is. This imperative underlies other normative assessments. It is the root of all value.

Because the real develops dialectically, the way the world appears and the way it really is differ—up to the moment that the "end" (*telos*) of the process is achieved. Then the distinction between appearance and reality is dissolved—or rather, reconstituted—in a thoroughly transparent way. But at the penultimate moment in this process, the apparent and the real diverge diametrically; the world as it appears is the *inverse* of the reality it expresses. This was how Feuerbach viewed Right Hegelian theology. "God makes man," the core principle of their theology, articulates the opposite (inverse) of what is really the case—that "man makes God." Feuerbach then went on to maintain that this discovery, when fully elaborated and installed in human consciousness, lays bare fundamental truths about essential humanity, establishing transparency where previously opacity had reigned.

The intellectual tendency that Feuerbach's contemporary, Auguste Comte (1798–1857) called "positivism" (to contrast with "negativism," his pejorative description of Hegel's "negations" and "negations of negations") is anti-Hegelian in each of these respects. In place of holism, it acknowledges the reality of natural kind divisions and assumes that there are distinct explanations for each discrete kind. Instead of endorsing extrascientific ways of knowing, positivism maintains that scientific knowledge is the only kind there is. It therefore rejects the dialectical method and the extrascientific truths it purports to establish. Finally, it supports a fact/value distinction, dissociating views about what is from judgments about what ought to be.

Durkheim was not literally a follower of Comte; hardly anyone was, more than a half century after Comte's death. But Durkheim's social theory falls within the larger positivist tradition. He was committed to explaining religion in its own right, without reference to any other natural kind or any overarching totality; he sought to explain it scientifically, without recourse to extrascientific methodologies; and his account of religion's elementary forms is ostensibly value-free. In these respects, Durkheim's purchase on religious phenomena differed fundamentally from Feuerbach's.

In his preface to *The Philosophy of Right* (1821), Hegel famously declared that "the owl of Minerva takes flight only with the setting of the sun." The philosopher's task, represented by the owl of Minerva, the symbol of wisdom, is to gain insight by discovering meanings that only become evident after they are realized—in other words, from the perspective of their "end" (*telos*). The Young Hegelians agreed. For "irreligious criticism" to reveal the fundamental truths they claimed it did, it was necessary that there be as evolved an account of religiosity as can be. By their lights, the Protestant theology they subjected to criticism satisfied this requirement. Religion has existed from time immemorial. Abrahamic religions have existed for more than two and a half millennia, and over the course of their existence, they have undergone profound transformations. Like everything else that expresses the nature of the real, these developments have had a generally progressive character; they represent movement towards the end (*telos*). Some religions are therefore more "advanced" than others, and one in particular, Lutheran Protestantism, is the most advanced of all.

Hegel's, and therefore Feuerbach's, view of more and less advanced religions was uncontroversial in philosophical circles in Protestant Germany in Feuerbach's time. It was taken for granted that monotheism represented a major advance over polytheism, and that the only religions worth taking seriously are the religions of the West—of Athens, Rome, and Jerusalem. It was also assumed that, among the Abrahamic religions, Christianity was superior to Judaism and Islam. Hegel imported these assumptions into his philosophy of history. But he did more than just accept the consensus view; he defended it, or rather the part of it that puts Lutheranism at the summit of religious thought.

In promoting the idea of a transcendent God, Judaism "negated" pagan notions of gods with human characteristics and dispositions. Pagan gods were in the world; the Jewish God was beyond it. With its core belief in Christ's incarnation, Christianity negated the negation. Its defining claim is that a transcendent God became flesh and lived for a while as a man. Because it is committed to this irreducibly paradoxical belief, it "supersedes" the pagan/Jewish opposition by constituting a higher unity that incorporates the "truth" of both.

Like other Europeans of their time, Hegelians thought Islam not worth taking seriously, notwithstanding its comparatively recent origin. The Muslim conception of God asserts his transcendence while denying Christ's divinity. It therefore marks a move away from, not towards, the end of history. For

Muslims, Jesus was only a prophet, and not the last or most authoritative one at that. That role falls to Mohammed, a figure Christian Europe had despised from the moment Islam erupted on the scene thirteen centuries earlier. Jews deny Christ's divinity too, but their problem is stubbornness and willful blindness. Judaism played a role in history's movement towards its end. Islam, on the other hand, is a retrograde phenomenon, a detour from history's course.

Within Christianity, the Young Hegelians were also confident, as was Hegel, that Protestantism was more advanced than Catholicism, and that the Protestant theologians whose positions they translated into the philosophical anthropology Feuerbach developed were more right about what religious experience involves than their predecessors or rivals. Their theology was crucial for developing a true philosophical anthropology because it represents the highest form of religious discourse. And, as its meaning is brought to light, so is the meaning of less developed forms of religious life. For to explain religion, or indeed anything at all, one must proceed, as it were, from the top down—from the most fully realized or developed expressions of forms of experience to more primitive forms.

Durkheim's explanatory strategy was diametrically opposed. He too had a notion of higher or more advanced forms of religiosity. But, for him, more advanced religions are not truer or closer to the real; they are only more complex. Like other positivists, Durkheim believed that to explain complex phenomena, it is necessary to identify the basic elements out of which they are constructed, and then to see how these

elements combine and evolve. Understanding proceeds from
the simple to the complex; from the bottom up.

Therefore to understand the Abrahamic religions and, by
implication, to account for their tenacity, it is first necessary to
explain the most elementary or simple forms of religious life.
Although Durkheim was ahead of his contemporaries in dis-
puting self-congratulatory notions of "primitiveness," he did
assume that the most simple or elementary forms of religious
life are those of peoples who are commonly designated primitive. *The Elementary Forms of Religious Life* reports, accordingly,
on the religious practices and beliefs of aboriginal peoples in
Australia and, less often, the Americas. Aboriginal Australian
and Amerindian religions have no direct historical connection
with Judaism, Christianity, or Islam. But Durkheim assumed
that religious ideas and practices evolve in basically the same
way everywhere. This is why he believed that the aboriginal
religions that ethnographers in his time were able to investigate directly are relevantly similar to the extinct and therefore
inaccessible religions of the Euroasian peoples whose ideas
and practices did develop into the Abrahamic faiths.

Comte rejected the Hegelian idea that history moves
through affirmations, negations, and negations of negations.
But, with deliberate irony, he too discerned an overarching
triadic structure in human history. He maintained that history
can be divided into pretheistic, theistic, and post-theistic (scientific, secular) stages. Needless to say, the similarity is superficial. In Hegel's view, history advances towards its "end" (*telos*)
through the unfolding of an inexorable internal dynamic.
There is nothing analogous in Comte's account. What moves

history along, in Comte's view, is a "natural," though not inevitable, sequencing of ideas and practices. Comte told what amounts to a "one thing leads to another" story guided by nothing more than plausible intuition. Theism or, more exactly, forms of civilization that accord with a theistic world-view, arose as a natural development of pretheistic ways of thinking and being. Scientific secularism will arise the same way as the old order becomes increasingly untenable—in other words, as news of what Nietzsche called God's "death" takes hold.

*   *   *

For Feuerbach, the "essence" of Christianity and therefore of religion generally was the human essence. Durkheim too claimed to have discovered the essence of religion—not through criticism of its highest form, but by investigating its most elementary manifestations. Implicit in his explanatory strategy is an objective that Hegelians, and therefore Young Hegelians, believed superseded, but that (most) philosophers and scientists have upheld from ancient times to the present: the search for "real definitions." For Durkheim, the essence of religion is not any deeper metaphysical (ultimately, human) truth, but a set of necessary and sufficient conditions that all and only religions satisfy. It is far from obvious that religion has an essence in this sense. The phenomena we designate by the word could have nothing fundamental in common. Religions would then bear, at most, a "family resemblance" to one another. If so, the religions of aboriginal Australia might be so different from the monotheistic religions that emerged in the ancient Near East that there is nothing to be learned about the latter by investigating the former. Durkheim thought otherwise. It was his view that all religions, elementary or not, share a common essence. This is a claim about the social world, not a report on how the word is used. Whether or not religion has an essence is a matter of fact, discoverable by assessing pertinent data.

Durkheim found that the essence of religion has nothing to do with beliefs in "supernatural" beings—in gods or God. This is impossible, he argued, because the very idea of the supernatural presupposes a distinction between nature and what lies outside or beyond it, a distinction that primitive peoples did not make. Religions are religions because there is a more abstract structural property that they share.

How a term should be defined is one thing; what it denotes—picks out in the world—is in principle something else. There is a connection, however, inasmuch as the aim of those who look for real definitions is to discover necessary and sufficient conditions for the usual denotations of terms. Should Durkheim's account of the essence of religion diverge significantly from ordinary usage, one could question whether it was indeed "religion" that he defined. On the other hand, real definitions can force changes in the way terms are used. This is the case with Durkheim's account of religion. There is nothing unusual in this; it is one of the ways that conceptual changes come about through progress in science. People used to think that whales are fish because they thought that fish are animals that live under water and that, though varying in size, look more or less the same in shape and other external characteristics. With progress in the biological sciences, a better understanding of "fishness" emerged. It became clear that the word had sometimes been used to designate creatures that are not fish—for example, whales. Durkheim thought that he had discovered a similar mistake in ordinary understandings of religion.

Nevertheless, real definitions are always constrained to some extent by common understandings of a term's denotation. This was what Durkheim assumed when he claimed that aboriginal "religions"—and therefore the more advanced religions that replaced them throughout most of the world—acknowledge a categorical and mutually exclusive division of lived experience into two realms: the *sacred* and the *profane*. The realm of the profane is the ordinary, workaday world. The realm of the sacred is vested with meanings that transcend the ordinary and that are experienced as if they constitute an altogether more significant order of being. Durkheim claimed that all religions make this distinction somehow, and that they all regulate relations between these distinct and independent realms. It is because they do that they are religions, as distinct from nonreligious systems of beliefs or forms of practice.

Here is what he wrote about the sacred and profane and the universality of the distinction:

> Whether simple or complex, all known religious beliefs display a common feature: They presuppose a classification of the real or ideal things that men conceive into two classes—two opposite genera—that are widely designated by two distinct terms, which the words *profane* and *sacred*

translate fairly well. The division of the world into two domains, one containing all that is sacred and the other all this is profane—such is the distinctive trait of religious thought. Beliefs, myths, dogmas and legends are either representations of systems of representations that express the nature of sacred things, the virtues and powers attributed to them, their history, and the relations with one another as well as with profane things. Sacred things are not simply those personal beings that are called gods or spirits. A rock, a tree, a spring, a pebble, a piece of wood, a house, in a word anything, can be sacred.

Durkheim distinguished *beliefs*, "states of opinion" consisting of "representations," from *rites*, "particular modes of action" shaped by beliefs. Both accord with the categorical distinction that marks religions off from other social phenomena.

> A rite can have sacredness; indeed there is no rite that does not have it to some degree. There are words, phrases, and formulas that can be said only by consecrated personages; there are gestures and movements that cannot be executed by just anyone....[4]

Sacredness is a social, not a natural, property. There is nothing in sacred things or in the ways they appear to human beings— in rocks, trees, springs, and the rest—in virtue of which they have a sacred dimension. The same holds for the profane. What sorts beliefs and rites into one or the other category are social practices that supervene on nature, giving rise to facts that are distinctively and irreducibly social.

What counts as sacred and profane will vary from society to society and can evolve over time within particular societies. Durkheim's contention is just that some sacred/profane distinction is indispensable for turning collections of individuals into human societies. Norms, shared understandings and values, that foster an overriding sense of group solidarity— not just to the individuals who, at particular moments, comprise the group, but to past and future group members as well—hold societies together. If Durkheim was right, a categorical distinction between the sacred and the profane structures these norms and sustains them. Therefore, wherever human societies exist, religions exist too. We always have had and always will have religions. It could not be otherwise.

This is a claim about structure, not substance. In principle, the ways sacred and profane realms are constituted can be as varied as the individuals who construct them through their social practices. However, Durkheim did think that there are discernible patterns in the evolution of human religions; he thought that they fall roughly into the schema Comte had proposed.

* * *

Durkheim believed that the reason why the sacred/profane distinction is a social universal has to do with its *function*, which is always to constitute self-regulating systems— supraindividual organisms, so to speak—comprised of otherwise independent individuals. By dividing the world, unconsciously and nondeliberately, into distinct and mutually exclusive realms, one of which is invested with special significance, the constituents of these systems make sense (to themselves) of their communal interactions. In this way, they become joined together by socially constructed meanings that they all acknowledge and that express the nature of their communal existence. This is why, as Durkheim put it, all religions are "true in their own way." [5] He did not mean that the claims they advance are literally true; quite the contrary—almost without exception, they are false. But they always *express* a deeper "truth." Feuerbach thought so too; but, again, the similarity is only superficial. For Feuerbach, all religions express the same truth about essential humanity, though with varying degrees of perspicuity. For Durkheim, there are as many truths as there are religions; truths about the core assumptions of groups constituted by sacred/profane categorizations of the world.

In short, Durkheim made two claims: that all religions acknowledge a categorical distinction between the sacred and profane; and that religions, so conceived, hold societies together. These are empirical hypotheses; what makes them true, if indeed they are, can only be matters of fact. It is therefore possible that religions have no essence or that their essence is different from the one Durkheim identified; only the facts of the matter rule out these possibilities. Similarly, there is no *a priori* reason to deny that something other than religion holds societies together or that having a common religion is just one way, among others, that societies cohere.

However, Durkheim sometimes equivocated, suggesting, though not in so many words, that his argument is a transcendental one; in other words, that it shows not just what is the case but also what must be.[6] Were this so, the ethnographic reports he relied upon to discover religion's essential property were not exactly data for empirical generalizations, but illustrations of a necessary *conceptual* connection between beliefs and practices organized around a core categorical distinction and an indispensable social function. These ways of understanding his findings are inconsistent, and, to the extent he suggested the latter, he can be reproached for misrepresenting what is ultimately an empirical argument only.

*   *   *

Durkheim's account of religion's structure and function implies that there is no necessary connection between the sacred and the godly. Gods entered human consciousness, and the "collective consciousness" of human societies, by a natural progression that begins with the beliefs and rites of primitive peoples. As in the more general Comtean theory of history, no endogenous developmental logic governs the course of change.[7] Therefore, unlike religion itself, ideas of gods or God are in principle avoidable. They do not figure in the most primitive religions; and neither, positivists expect, will they figure in the next and final epochal stage of humankind's social existence.

One could even say, on Durkheimean grounds, that the post-theistic religions of the future are already far along in the process of formation; and that, with important exceptions, the theistic religions that presently coexist with them no longer serve the function they once did. It would not refute Durkheim's contentions if those superannuated religions were to survive indefinitely so long as they play no role in maintaining social cohesion. Then, if they survive, it would be for reasons that no longer pertain to their original function—most likely, for psychological or even political reasons. Were this possibility to come to fruition, Judaism, Christianity, and Islam would not count as religions in Durkheim's sense, though they would probably continue to be called religions in colloquial speech.

*   *   *

The story Durkheim told in *The Elementary Forms* begins with a phenomenon of considerable interest to early twentieth century thinkers: *totemism*. Europeans first identified this form of religiosity in North American Indian societies; the word is of Ojibwa origin. It soon became apparent that "primitive" peoples elsewhere held similar beliefs, and that traces of totemic practices persist to this day, even in the so-called world religions that replaced the beliefs and practices Durkheim described. Durkheim claimed, uncontroversially, that clans are the primordial social grouping, and that they characteristically attribute their origin to a totem, an animal or other nonhuman being. The group, then, identifies with its imagined founder, whose "spirit" serves as a source of communal renewal. Totemic beliefs are usually accompanied by origin myths that supply the ideational content for a distinction between the sacred and the profane. They explain how and why the totem is sacred, and how and why its realm should be regulated through rites and other rituals. Violations of these regulations are *taboo*—forbidden. Like totemic beliefs, taboos are mental representations. They may be, and often are, coercively enforced by political, religious, or patriarchal authorities. But even when they are not, they are internalized and vested with affective significance. The cohesiveness of the group and its survival into the future depend upon their observance.

Decades later, Claude Lévi-Strauss, an even more determined structuralist than Durkheim and also a more determined opponent of the idea that primitive thought is inferior to or even qualitatively different from the thinking of more advanced peoples (logic and mathematics aside), ventured to explain the origins of totemism in a way that complements Durkeim's account.[8] Lévi-Strauss held that human cognition is based on analogical thinking and that, at a level of abstraction appropriate for discerning universal truths about human nature, it follows fixed structural forms. However, the ways structures are implemented depend on historically contingent circumstances. Because "primitive" peoples interact with nature without the aid of technologies that come with the advance of civilization, their situations are, by modern standards, precarious. They are therefore desperately in need of secure understandings of their situation and their prospects. Totemic beliefs provide an accessible organizing principle for the analogies they, like all human beings, rely upon. Totemism makes sense of the world through the imposition of comprehensive classificatory schemes. It is therefore continuous with modern science; totemic systems are proto-scientific theories that explain phenomena as well as possible, given what totemists know and given the absence of developed symbolic thinking. Lévi-Strauss's speculations about the rise of totemism and his assessment of its fundamental rationality address issues Durkheim did not explore. Durkheim only insisted on the ubiquity of the phenomenon at the dawn of human civilization; and on how, since the first social groups were clans, collectivities based on kinship, clans became the locus of totemic spirits.

The totem had a distinctive personality, but it was the personality of the collectivity, not of the individuals who comprised it. In time, though, as individuality asserted itself within the group, it became natural to think of the group's personality—or rather, instantiations of it—as resident within its constituent members, in their bodies and minds. By this train of thought, the idea that individuals possess *souls*—non- or extranatural entities, located in individuals, connected with but not identical to their bodies or minds yet central to, indeed definitive of, their identities—arose nearly everywhere. This is an individualistic, not a communal, notion. But, if Durkheim was right, its origins lie in modes of thinking that express the identities of social groups. The soul idea has been entrenched in human cultures since prehistoric times, and has survived the transition from pretheistic to theistic forms of thought. All the theological religions, including the Abrahamic ones, incorporate and adapt it in their own ways.[9]

Clans are more long-lived than their members. Individuals are born into clans, which exist before their members do. Clans also survive their members' deaths—provided, of course, that the group itself survives. Totemic spirits persist correspondingly. It is natural, therefore, to suppose that individuated souls are similarly persistent. Thus arose the belief that what one *really* is survives death and, in some belief systems, precedes birth as well.[10] In short, souls are *immortal*. In premonotheistic systems of religious ideation, immortality is a defining property of divinity, of godliness. The soul, however, is not a god. For that concept to emerge, the thought that the soul idea expresses must be extended in such a way that people are able to think of souls, or soul-like beings, with personalities unconnected to the personalities of mortals. Gods are souls freed from the taint of humanity. But the idea is a natural extension of a more ancient idea tied intimately to notions of human individuality. This is why where souls are, gods will surely, though not inevitably, follow.[11]

In sum, there is a trajectory that begins with totemism and ends with theism, or at least with polytheism, propelled along by intuitively plausible extensions of earlier ideas. At the root of this process is a transhistorical, inherently human quest for meaning. Totemic beliefs and practices arose because primitive peoples, banded together into groups based on kinship, endeavored to make sense of the tensions between the collectivities they constituted and the environments they inhabited. In due course, the totem evolved into a spirit which, when individuated, became a soul. Because souls are personalities and because they are immortal, this notion gave rise, in turn, to notions of gods. But then, if there are gods who, though immortal, are more or less like human beings, they, like human beings, would themselves constitute social groups; and these groups, like human groups, would be hierarchically structured.

Thus the idea arose that some gods are more godlike—greater and more powerful—than others, and that the greater gods rule over the lesser ones. The next step is almost irresistible: it is to suppose that, within polytheistic hierarchies, one god emerges supreme. Inasmuch as (most) human communities have supreme leaders; why would it not also be the case in the heavens (or in whatever realm the gods inhabit)?

The transition from a supreme god to One God was also an intuitively plausible extension of a received idea. But this "advance" required more of a leap than the others. Eventually, most of the world's peoples did become monotheists. But this seldom happened spontaneously. Monotheism was introduced, often coercively, by proselytizing Christians or Muslims and, in pre-Christian times, by sects of proselytizing Jews.

Comte's account of history's epochal stages does not end with monotheism, and neither does the Comtean story it is fair to impute to Durkheim. In time, as enlightenment spreads and the implausibility of the God idea becomes increasingly apparent, the One God will go the way of his ancestor divinities, and humankind will enter into a secular (post-theistic) age. Theism—along with its more austere cousin, deism—are therefore only phases in the history of religious thought. These epochal forms have survived for a very long time but, in the end, they too will pass, as surely as totemism has.

Thus positivists, like Durkheim, and Hegelians, like Feuerbach, are more in accord than one might at first suppose. For Durkheim, what motivates the trajectory that leads from totemism to God and beyond was what the Young Hegelians also believed central to theism and to its future: a quest for meaning in a world that is ultimately uncaring, burdensome, and meaningless. Durkheim was a naturalist, though not always a consistent one; Feuerbach was not. Mired in a metaphysical framework peculiar to classical German philosophy, he saw the quest for meaning as a metaphysical condition that would end when individuals take consciousness of a true, philosophical anthropology. For Durkheim, the need to make sense of the human condition—its social aspects, especially—was a bedrock, trans-social and transhistorical psychological fact. Nevertheless, they came to similar conclusions about faith's transitory role in human history. They both thought that the age of theism would pass and that then transparency will reign. For the Young Hegelians, this moment would come at history's end; for Durkheim, it is the final outcome of a contingent, though "natural" and all but inexorable, sequence of events.

*   *   *

Belief is an individual matter; it is individuals, not social groups, who hold beliefs. When their beliefs are irrational, their existence and even more glaringly their persistence invite psychological explanations. This is as it should be. Nevertheless, there is a *social* dimension to religious life that investigators ignore at their peril. It was Durkheim's view that this dimension is key to understanding religion generally, and therefore, by implication, not only the emergence of theism but also its persistence in the face of confutation and ultimately its career in a world where faith in God is bad faith. From a vantage point abstract enough for the common features of Durkheimean positivism and Feuerbachian "negativism" to become apparent, it is fair to say that Feuerbach would have agreed—that, for him too, religion, like other manifestations of what Hegel called "absolute spirit," is, in the final analysis, a social thing. He would also have agreed with Durkheim's insistence that "all religions are true"—in the sense that they all express, though in a distorted way, what is of paramount human concern.

Finally, Feuerbach and Durkheim would agree that when history has reached the point where most people see the world aright, aspects of religiosity will remain. With transparency achieved, the world will not become duller as in the mechanistic vision of eighteenth century materialists; it will be no less enchanted. They would agree, in other words, that the affective dimension of the Abrahamic religions does not depend on the *content* of their beliefs, and certainly not on their support for the existence of God, but on their genuine, though distorted, recognition of the sacred dimension of humankind's social existence. The Abrahamic religions can and typically do have deleterious effects. But if the human race manages to outlast their tenure, then, in time, these causes of discontent and harm will dissolve into the light of day. Theism—or rather, monotheism—will by then have lost not just its social but also its psychological function. It will have become a historical memory like the pagan faiths that preceded it. When this much-anticipated outcome finally comes to pass, nothing worthwhile will have been lost, and much will be gained.

CHAPTER THREE

THE TENACITY OF
AN ILLUSION

Feuerbach explained religion by *interpreting* a representation of its "highest" form. To this end, he "translated"
the theological concepts of the Right Hegelians into anthropological concepts that purport to represent the truth about
essential humanity. The translation metaphor is instructive,
but also misleading. Translations go from one already existing
language to another. In Feuerbach's case, only one of the "languages," Right Hegelianism, existed prior to the translation
itself. The concepts that reveal its meaning—and therefore
the essence of Christianity and ultimately the human
essence—had to be discovered as the translation proceeded.

To be sure, Feuerbach was not completely in the dark.
Drawing on Hegel and the broader anthropological strain of
post-Kantian German philosophy, he knew in a general way
what essential humanity was. However it was Right Hegelian
theology, which Feuerbach systematized and then translated
from, that contributed most to the construction of the anthropological language he translated it *into*. Theology could play
this role because the referents of its concepts, being immaterial and therefore unreal, were pure objectifications; because
there is nothing to them except the meanings they invert.

Feuerbach thought that this program would be emancipatory, that it would free humankind from religion, because he thought that when the meanings of religious concepts are grasped, their (unreal) objects disappear. By taking consciousness of the fact that man makes God, the insubstantiality of the God idea becomes salient, we see God as a pure objectification of our own essential traits, and we are liberated from God's thrall. Thus criticism both explains and liberates. This is another respect in which the translation metaphor is misleading. Languages normally survive translation. The language of the Right Hegelians does not; it is reduced away along with the objectifications it represents.

Feuerbach attempted to make sense of religion by reflecting upon it from the standpoint of its end (*telos*) or purpose. His account of Christianity's essence was therefore teleological. Teleological explanations were the mainstay of medieval (Aristotelian) science. But as long ago as the seventeenth century, the founders of modern science and philosophy rejected teleological explanations in the natural sciences and, along with them, the idea that natural phenomena signify or mean anything. They maintained that in nature there are no "final causes," as Aristotle called ends; that nature is *meaningless*. But in nature everything does have what Aristotle called an "efficient cause." By this, Aristotle meant roughly what we mean by "cause" today. To explain a phenomenon is therefore to show how it came about, not to reveal what it means from the vantage point of its end; it means nothing, and there are no ends. Modern science accordingly adopted a working hypothesis that found immediate vindication in the new physics of the seventeenth century: that nature is governed by universal causal principles or "laws," and that to explain a phenomenon is to subsume it under the laws that determine it. Interpreting the world, showing what it means, ceased to be the aim of the sciences of nature. The aim became instead to discover nature's causal structure.

*   *   *

There is a sense in which, like Feuerbach, Freud too was an interpreter. His theory of the unconscious, psychoanalysis, underwrites a therapeutic practice based on interpretations of patients' utterances and behaviors. Moreover, psychoanalytic interpretations too are emancipatory. By taking consciousness of their unconscious beliefs and desires, both cognitively and affectively, patients are freed from their thrall. Freud provided psychoanalytic interpretations of cultural phenomena as well—including religion. In this respect too, his position resembles Feuerbach's. Feuerbachian criticism aimed to emancipate humankind from religious beliefs. In a similar vein, Freud seems to have thought that when people come to understand the psychological bases of their theistic convictions, these convictions will pass. However, Freud had a more realistic view than Feuerbach of the social and political consequences of this realization. Feuerbach and the other Young Hegelians thought that irreligious criticism would unleash a social and political revolution. Freud held no similar view. His political inclinations were progressive but not revolutionary, and he was anything but optimistic about civilization's prognosis.[1]

In this respect, Freud was more like Durkheim than

Feuerbach, and this is not their only similarity. Notwithstanding his reliance on interpretive methodologies, Freud's general theoretical orientation was, in fact, closer to Durkheim's than to Feuerbach's. Psychoanalytic practice does aim to discover meanings, but the meanings it uncovers are always relative to particular persons or groups; they are not inherent in the phenomena under investigation and they play no role in any grand metaphysical narrative. The meanings of interest to Freud are brought into being and sustained by "efficient causes," and are therefore explicable in just the ways that modern science allows. It was as a scientist, not a metaphysician, that Freud turned his attention to religion. He took it for granted that, being part of nature broadly construed, religious phenomena have causes that are discoverable in principle, and that the only way to make sense of them is to discover what these causes are. In *The Future of an Illusion* (1927), Freud addressed some of these phenomena, focusing particularly on the question that each of our authors puzzled over at least implicitly—why theistic convictions are so resistant to rational confutation, and why they survive and even flourish in the modern era, despite awareness of their untenability.

* * *

Feuerbach and Durkheim were each, in their own way, concerned with religion as such. Freud advanced no view about what religion is in general. Also, unlike *The Essence of Christianity* and *The Elementary Forms of Religious Life*, *The Future of an Illusion* has nothing to say about "essences," much less essences of some or all religions. Freud's aim was only to account for theism's (unconscious) appeal.

Although Freud shied away from advertising his disapproval, it is hard not to read *The Future of an Illusion* as an indictment of theism. But it is not obvious what Freud's objection is. Part of the problem is that, from a logical point of view, a causal explanation for a belief's appeal that has nothing to do with rational standards for belief acceptance does not by itself impugn the belief. A reason-irrelevant causal explanation for the appeal of theistic beliefs would not embarrass theism if it could be established that theism is true. The point is a general one. It is demonstrable, according to the most exacting standards, that "$2 + 2 = 4$." Perhaps some day there will be an unimpeachable account of the human capacity to grasp this truth, and to find it intuitive. Such an account would explain, among other things, why the belief that "$2 + 2 = 4$" is difficult to dislodge. But it would not impugn the belief's truth. It would only explain why even mathematically untutored people are inclined to believe it, whether or not they trust the authorities who assure them that it is true, and whether or not they would (or could) understand the reasons these authorities can adduce in its support. Were it possible to prove that God exists or even to establish the likelihood that he does, the situation would be similar. Then the fact, if it is a fact, that human beings are inclined to believe in God for reason-irrelevant causes would in no way diminish the claim. But since rational theology does not succeed in establishing the rationality of belief in God, a psychological explanation for the belief's appeal can threaten "God exists" in a way that no reason-irrelevant causal explanation could threaten "2 + 2 = 4."

*   *   *

In much the way that *The Elementary Forms of Religious Life* aimed not just to explain religion but also to support a view about the nature of human societies and about the need for sociological explanations for social facts, Freud's depiction of theism as an *illusion* was part of a larger theoretical—and practical (therapeutic)—project. It depends on and supports psychoanalysis, the theory of human psychology Freud invented. For much of the twentieth century, this larger project reverberated throughout the intellectual culture. It remains a presence to this day. Classical psychoanalysis and its close descendants still have active adherents and elements of psychoanalytic theory survive in nonpsychoanalytic theories and forms of clinical practice. But, in comparison to the situation several decades ago, psychoanalysis has fallen out of favor, and it is fair to expect that its influence will continue to wane. Whether or not this is a welcome turn of events need not concern us because it is unnecessary, for the present purpose, to defend Freud's theory of the unconscious or even to delve into many of its important contentions. It will suffice only to recount what is needed to explain what Freud meant when he described theism as an "illusion," and what that description implies.

Psychoanalysis was always a work in progress, changing as clinical practice and other investigative techniques brought new evidence to light. But two very general aspects of Freud's position never changed: his acceptance of the "folk psychological" conviction that beliefs and desires explain behavior, and his contention that some of these beliefs and desires can be, and importantly are, unconscious.

Throughout the history of science, "folk" theories, rooted in common sense and pervasive cultural understandings, have been superseded by more developed theories, using different concepts and explanatory strategies. Psychological explanations of behavior are still very much in a "folk" stage: the idea that beliefs and desires explain behavior has been an unchallenged assumption until quite recently, and it is still the majority view. Psychoanalytic theory falls within the broad folk psychological ambit. Freud's account of the nature of beliefs and desires was hardly standard, but he never questioned the assumption that beliefs and desires, properly conceived, are explanatory in the way that most people have always taken for granted.

On the other hand, his case for the determinative role of unconscious beliefs and desires was anything but standard. Partly thanks to Freud, the idea is now ensconced in the common sense of our intellectual culture. Perhaps it has never been remote from ordinary understandings. But the idea is at odds with longstanding philosophical conceptions of the mind—going back, at least, to the origins of modern philosophy four centuries ago. Descartes's position, briefly encountered in chapter one, played a seminal role in this development.

In his *Meditations on First Philosophy*, Descartes set out to find foundations for the emerging sciences of nature. To this end, he developed a methodological strategy with momentous consequences. He resolved to regard as real—to admit into his ontology—only what can be *known* to exist; and he resolved, in turn, to admit only those knowledge claims that are logically impossible to doubt or, should he be successful in finding (indubitable) certainties, beliefs that are derived from these foundations. Descartes's declared intention was to rebut skepticism, a philosophical position and frame of mind that he believed dangerous to both science and religion. Thus he set out to demonstrate that there is no need, in general, to suspend judgment about the findings of the new sciences of nature or, not unrelatedly, to entertain doubts about the existence of God. To these ends, he devised a more radical skepticism than the one he would combat. The skepticism he proposed mandates not merely that we suspend judgment on the truth or falsity of claims about which we harbor doubts, but something more demanding: it requires that we regard as false whatever is logically possible to doubt.

Needless to say, holding beliefs to this standard would be impossible in active life; one could not do anything if one doubted everything. However, the skepticism Descartes proposed, Cartesian skepticism, is feasible in contemplative contexts. As all students of philosophy know, Descartes concluded that only one belief passes this test: that "I exist." The so-called *cogito* argument through which he defended this position, "I think therefore I am" (*cogito ergo sum*), is the best-known and most studied argument in the history of philosophy. Its rationale, in brief, is that it is logically impossible to doubt that "I think" when and insofar as I do think (cogitate)

—because doubting that I think is itself a kind of thinking (cogitation). Descartes's argument meets the standards his methodology requires. But, strictly speaking, all it establishes is that "there is thinking."

Descartes thought that it establishes more than this—that the thinking (cogitating) that one cannot doubt is in some pertinent sense one's own; that there is something that thinks, which he identified with the self and called *I*; and, most important of all (for using this existence claim as the basis for rebutting skepticism about science and religion) that the *I* that thinks is a *unitary consciousness* that exists continuously for a period of time, even as its contents, Descartes called them "ideas," change. In advancing these positions, Descartes effectively replaced logically unassailable arguments with rational intuitions. It is tempting to see a diminution of rigor in this (unacknowledged) change of method. Perhaps so. But had he abided by his declared methodological constraint, he would not have been able to move beyond "there is thinking"; and he would therefore have had no way to reintroduce science and religion, much less to defend them against skeptical attacks. However, Descartes had a better reason for relaxing the stringency of the skepticism he concocted. That reason is suggested by his calling his reflections on "first philosophy" (basic metaphysics) *meditations*. What he recorded in the text in question was not just a series of logical arguments. It was also a report on the ways Cartesian skepticism transformed his own state of mind when and insofar as he meditated on ontology, on what is, from its perspective.

Cartesian skepticism is susceptible to a mechanistic construal: submit an existence claim or, as Descartes himself did in *The Meditations*, a category of existence claims—for example, judgments based on sense perception—to the test. If it is possible to be wrong, the claim fails and must therefore be regarded as false unless and until it is reinstated by rationally compelling arguments that ground it on indubitable foundations. However, the skepticism Descartes deployed also has a psychological or "meditative" aspect. It purges the mind of prejudgments about the real, so that inferences that are genuinely self-evident present themselves with overwhelming force, compelling assent. Ordinary life conditions us to believe that nearly everything with which we interact is real. We could hardly negotiate our way through life if we thought otherwise; anyone who genuinely did doubt everything that is possible to doubt would be in the grip of a profoundly incapacitating paranoia. But, if Descartes was right, one must assume precisely this state of mind for the quest for certainty to succeed. This is why he famously imagined that there was an evil demon bent on deceiving him—a godlike but malevolent creature, powerful enough to deceive him about that which, prereflectively, seems most certain. He invoked the evil demon to get his mind in the right condition to make proper use of rational intuitions. By making himself believe that an evil demon is deceiving him, Descartes purged himself of unwarranted prejudgments about the real, leaving his mind receptive to recognizing whatever genuinely is self-evident. On this basis, Descartes concluded that he could know, with as much certainty as he knows that there is thinking, that this thinking is his own, that he is a thinking thing (a mind), and that his mind and his consciousness are one and the same. Inasmuch as each and every thought one thinks is one's own, the *I* has direct access only to its own mind. But that is enough, Descartes maintained, to ground the claims advanced in the emerging sciences of nature and in religion.[2]

The "I" that exists is a temporally continuous site of ever-changing "ideas" (or impressions)—including beliefs and desires. But then beliefs and desires are and can only be conscious. The very idea of *unconscious* beliefs and desires is, from the standpoint of Cartesian philosophy, oxymoronic. This had been the mainstream philosophical view for centuries before Freud. Psychoanalytic theory challenged this consensus and overturned it.

Freud argued for unconscious beliefs and desires—and therefore against identifying the mind with consciousness—in much the way that Durkheim argued for the reality of social facts that are irreducible to facts about individuals. Durkheim maintained that to explain, for example, differential suicide rates in European countries, as distinct from individual suicides, it is necessary to introduce irreducibly social notions such as *norms* and *anomie* (normlessness), and to regard them as real.[3] In much the same way, Freud maintained that to account for what psychoanalytic practice reveals about the maladies afflicting psychiatric patients, and to explain many cultural phenomena, it is necessary to regard unconscious beliefs and desires as real.

These are not pragmatic claims. The point, for both authors, is not that, given what we now know, or in order to simplify what would otherwise be too complex or too vast for human beings to grasp in real time, sociological explanations trump psychological explanations or that explanations that involve unconscious beliefs and desires trump (yet unknown) explanations consistent with the Cartesian doctrine that mind and consciousness are one. The contention, in both cases, is that the best explanations in principle for the phenomena in question involve factors of the sort Durkheim and Freud sought to establish. Both authors were largely successful in this endeavor, Freud especially. There are still philosophers and social scientists who believe that in principle sociology is reducible to psychology, and therefore that only pragmatic reasons can justify its continuation as an independent discipline, but hardly anyone nowadays is troubled by claims for the causal efficacy of unconscious beliefs and desires.

*　　*　　*

Freud's explanation for theism's appeal depends too on an account of the instinctual drives that motivate human beings' actions and thoughts. His findings are controversial, of course, but not in a way that puts his explanation in jeopardy. Yet again, Freud's views changed as his theory developed. For a long time, he held that the sole motivational force underlying human behavior is *libido*, a drive that is sexual (erotic) in nature. Accordingly, he set out to show how even the most refined, ostensibly nonsexual human achievements in the arts and sciences—including his own attempts to discover the secrets of the unconscious—are driven by a will rooted ultimately in a biological imperative to reproduce. But by the late

1920s, mounting evidence drawn from clinical practice and also, it seems, from reflections on political and cultural developments led Freud to amend this contention by claiming that, in addition to libido, there is also an aggressive or destructive instinctual drive—a death instinct (*thanatos*). Thanatos or, rather, the interaction of Thanatos and Eros figure prominently in *Civilization and Its Discontents*, a text that continues the argument of *The Future of an Illusion*. By 1927, when *The Future of an Illusion* was published, Freud was well on the way toward recasting his theory of instinctual drives. Nevertheless, a death instinct plays no role in the account of theism's appeal that Freud offered there. Perhaps he was not yet confident about what he was coming to believe. But there is a more satisfactory explanation. Freud did not need to join Thanatos with Eros to account for the etiology of *neuroses*, the key to understanding theism's appeal.

Freud's position starts from recognition of the fact that human infants undergo a protracted period of physical maturation during which they are helpless and therefore unable to act directly to realize their desires. The infant is dependent on others, normally the mother, for almost everything. But infants are as libidinally driven as human beings at later stages of life. This is why libidinal frustration is a determinative fact of human existence. The basic structures of the human mind or, at least, of its unconscious component are forged early in the maturation process through the collision of what Freud called "the pleasure principle"—untrammeled libido—and "the reality principle" with which it comes into conflict.[4]

This conflict accounts for the pessimistic view of the

human prospect that Freud articulated in *Civilization and Its Discontents*. By "civilization," Freud meant all the ways that human beings organize their collective existence and their struggles with nature. Civilization is indispensable not only for human flourishing but for survival itself. Yet civilization is possible only through the repression of instinctual drives. Paradoxically, it is libido that impels what human beings do to protect themselves from nature and from each other, but it is the frustration of libido that makes it possible for them to construct these protections. The unconscious is forged in these circumstances; it is therefore shaped by the frustrations that civilization requires. This is why, for all that we are able to achieve in technology and in the regulation of our collective affairs, happiness—or, at least, desire satisfaction, the primordial form of human happiness—lies forever beyond our reach. The quest for happiness can be and often is a powerful motivator, and efforts to achieve happiness can and sometimes do partially succeed. But, in the nature of things, they can never succeed well enough for civilization's "discontents" to be more than superficially and temporarily alleviated.

In view of the role libidinal frustration plays in causing discontents, one might suppose that the elimination of sexual repression would be a remedy. Some of Freud's contemporaries attributed this view to him, and the impression that he advocated sexual license lingers. But this was not the case. Because the frustration of instinctual drives is unavoidable in infancy and early childhood, enhanced sexual freedom for adults or for children as they become more capable of acting on their desires cannot alter the human condition fundamentally. Perhaps societies can do better in mitigating discontents than they now do or have ever done; and, no doubt, sexual frustrations would be reduced if societal prohibitions were relaxed. One could therefore argue, as Freud did not, that existing prohibitions are needlessly repressive.[5] But even the most enlightened sexual policies cannot rectify the unavoidable frustrations that shape the (unconscious) human mind.

Freud's insistence on the fact of infantile sexuality and all that follows from it accords with the Enlightenment imperative to face reality squarely; to "dare to know." But his position breaks with a facet of enlightened thought or, more exactly, with optimistic strains of it. Some enlightened thinkers in the eighteenth and early nineteenth centuries imagined that, with reason in control, happiness would finally come within reach. We would still be subject to the vicissitudes of life in an indifferent universe and to the travails associated with birth, maturation, decline, and death. But human causes of human misery would be eliminated, and the unhappiness caused by what cannot be eliminated would be diminished through technological and moral progress. The Young Hegelians espoused this sort of optimism. They believed that once the human meaning of theistic ideation was properly grasped, heaven or, more precisely, a humanly feasible approximation of that inherently theistic idea would be realized on earth; they believed, in short, in human perfectibility. Freud's findings challenged that aspiration, though not as thoroughly as might appear. Even as he made the case for the inexorability of our discontents, he lauded efforts to ameliorate the sorrows that we bring upon ourselves and that nature visits upon us.[6]

But, contrary to the hopes of Feuerbach and other enlightened thinkers, he insisted that no matter how beneficial such efforts may be, they can never undo the most fundamental causes of our discontent—because libidinal frustrations will always be with us and will always shape the unconscious mind. It was plainly Freud's view that, on balance, this is a good thing. Otherwise civilization itself, and therefore the technological and moral progress it sustains, without which human beings would be helpless against the forces of nature, would be impossible.

Freud's account of mental development, like much else in psychoanalytic theory, changed over the years, and has always been controversial even within psychoanalytic circles. But we can remain agnostic on the merits of contending Freudian or Freudian-inspired accounts of mental development and aloof from the debates Freud's work launched. It *is* necessary, however, to remark briefly on some very general Freudian positions. Because Freud's views are probably mistaken, even at the level of generality I will describe, his explanation for theism's tenacity may not ultimately be sustainable. But however that may be, it warrants attention because it provides a clear example of a naturalistic account of theistic belief that impugns theism beyond recuperation, even while not logically undermining its claim to truth.

Freud's version of this kind of argument stood alone for more than half a century. As noted at the outset, there have lately been stirrings of new research paradigms based in cognitive psychology and neuroscience that may at some point provide additional examples. But contemporary investigators who regard religion as a phenomenon susceptible to scientific inquiry have been more reluctant than Freud to draw antitheistic conclusions, even when their findings tend in that direction. Perhaps their work is based on sounder science, though this is far from certain. But, so far at least, their gloss on their (hardly conclusive) findings suggests that theism is somehow "hardwired" into the human mind.[7] This is obviously false, since there are many who do break free from theism's hold. For those who want to know what is wrong with "the opium of the people," it is also disabling. If the mental structures they hypothesize exist and if they constrain individuals' abilities to opt out of theism, their existence would relieve believers of responsibility for their beliefs, rendering charges of bad faith otiose. Freud's account suggests a different conclusion. It provides a template for illustrating how a reason-irrelevant psychological explanation can be enlisted in the struggle against bad faith and for good, and ultimately for overcoming faith altogether.

*   *   *

Psychoanalytic theory provides a narrative account of the emergence in infancy and childhood of a sense of the self (ego) and its place in nature. The process proceeds in overlapping stages. Exactly what these stages are and how they should be conceived has never quite been settled. For the present purpose, it will suffice to identify only two steps along the purported trajectory: the period of infantile narcissism and the Oedipal stage. Freudians have never wavered in their insistence that human beings must pass through these stages, emerging, in each case, with a sounder sense of self—that is, with a more realistic apprehension of the boundaries between the self and the other. For any of a variety of reasons, the developmental process can go wrong. Indeed, it almost always does go wrong to some extent. Moreover, no one emerges from it unscathed; "mental health" is therefore more of a regulative ideal, a goal we seek to reach or at least to approximate, than a condition we can fully attain.

At birth, the infant recognizes no distinction between the self and the other; it experiences itself as if it were one with the universe. But this "infantile narcissism" does not last for long. Inevitably, reality intrudes. The other is, at first, the primordial caregiver, the mother or mother figure. As the child matures, its awareness of other persons, and of the familial, social, and natural order into which it is inserted becomes more realistic. But the (male) infant's focus on the mother remains. In time, roughly when the child is between four and six years old, the Oedipal stage is reached. At that point, awareness of the boundaries between the self and the other is well enough developed that the child's desire for the mother is focused and direct. The father or father figure then becomes the child's rival—one with whom he cannot successfully compete. The child therefore wishes, impotently and unconsciously, to kill the father and to replace him. This ineluctable state of affairs gives rise to frustrations severe enough to cause the child to repress overt sexual desires for a time, and to direct them away from the primal caregiver. Thus, as the Oedipal stage draws to an end, the child enters into a "latency period" in which psychosexual development is frozen. This period lasts until puberty, when, for organic reasons, libidinal desires become irrepressible. As they reemerge, if all has gone well, the child directs his sexual interests outside the family sphere and engages in constructive, sociable activities that, though libidinal in origin, have nothing directly to do with sexuality or reproduction. When all goes less well, as is always the case to some extent, disorders of varying degrees of severity result.

This story is told from the standpoint of the male child. This is plainly a problem. But we can remain agnostic on the question of whether Freud or his followers or feminist critics who are otherwise sympathetic to psychoanalysis have succeeded in confecting a distinctively psychoanalytic account of the mental development of girls. It is an important question, but it does not affect the explanation for theism's tenacity that Freud advanced.

In the psychiatry of his time, as in ours, it was commonplace to distinguish *neuroses* from *psychoses*. Psychoses are more severe than neuroses. In Freud's lifetime and for many decades afterwards, until psychopharmacological treatments for brain disorders began to show promise, it was debatable within the psychiatric community whether psychoses were treatable at all. Even today, the consensus view is that, while their effects can be ameliorated, the underlying maladies that give rise to them are often incurable. It can seem that the difference is only one of degree. However, from a psychoanalytic perspective, the difference is qualitative. Neuroses and psychoses result from problems arising at different stages in the development of unconscious mental structures. Psychoses involve regression to infantile narcissism. Breakdowns in these most basic mental structures, the ones through which the self forges a primordial sense of its own identity and its difference from everything else, can be and often are elicited by crushing circumstances. But a condition for their possibility is always a defect in the structures themselves. Neuroses, on the other hand, do not reflect problems with the boundaries of the self. They owe their origin instead to unsatisfactory resolutions of Oedipal conflicts.

It was Freud's view that psychoanalytic practice, the talking therapy he pioneered, was effective only in the treatment of neuroses. Psychoses lie beyond its reach. The aim of psychoanalytic therapy was therefore to cure or at least ameliorate neuroses. By coming to understand the Oedipal origins of one's own maladies, not just cognitively but affectively as well, patients free themselves from their grip. As in Feuerbachian criticism, a thoroughgoing interpretive understanding that reaches the emotions as well as consciousness undoes oppressive and debilitating conditions.

It is convenient to think of the unconscious as an organ that develops in a more or less determined pattern as the organism in which it is ensconced matures. Its developmental trajectory is therefore largely fixed: barring exogenous interferences with the normal developmental path, infantile minds develop into adult minds just as infantile kidneys develop into adult kidneys. Anomalies, if they arise, occur at the margins; and, from an organic point of view, almost always involve comparatively minor discrepancies from the prescribed path. Nev-

ertheless, for the organisms in which they occur, their consequences can be momentous. This is the case with kidneys, and
it is the case with minds. Deviations from the normal path can
cause great suffering. They can even lead to death.

*   *   *

Although he was not always consistent in his usage, Freud
drew a distinction in *The Future of an Illusion* between *illusions*
and *delusions*, and then implicitly and orthogonally to the
former distinction, between true and false beliefs. The latter
distinction is hardly peculiar to psychoanalysis. In philosophical discussions reaching back to Greek antiquity (and,
implicitly, in the common sense of all peoples throughout history), the difference pertains to the truth values attributable to
beliefs. The belief that "God exists" is true if and only if God
exists; otherwise it is false. Although he never said so explicitly, even in *The Future of an Illusion* where it would have been
helpful to be more clear, it is fair to say that Freud, like most
enlightened thinkers, thought that "God exists" is false. But
this is not why God is an illusion. Illusions in Freud's sense
may be false and usually are. But it is not their falseness that
makes them illusions. Beliefs can be both illusory and true.

Illusions are expressions of unconscious desires. To say
that theism is an illusion is therefore to make a claim about
what causes people to believe that God exists or, more precisely, about why so many are so eager to accept that belief
and so reluctant to give it up. The claim is that the cause is an
unconscious desire. People believe that "God exists," when

111

they do, not because they have reason to think it true, but because they want it to be true—in a way that is not evident to the conscious mind. If Freud was right, theism would be an illusion even if "God exists" turned out to be true after all.

An illusion is a belief that one desires unconsciously to be true, held in the absence of plausible reasons. A delusion is a belief held to be true in the face of overwhelming evidence to the contrary. In *The Future of an Illusion*, Freud had little to say about delusions except that they too are expressions of unconscious desires. When people (consciously) believe, say, that they will become multimillionaires by winning a lottery— Freud's example was of a middle-class girl who believed that a prince would come to marry her—then, inasmuch as the probability of the belief turning out to be true is extremely low, the belief counts as an illusion, even in the very unlikely event that the desired result occurs. Illusions are beliefs based on "feelings" generated by unconscious desires. Delusions are illusions that rationally compelling reasons directly and overwhelmingly confute. If, for example, someone believes that she is a lottery winner or a princess, when she is not, she suffers from a delusion. She believes something that is obviously false that she unconsciously wants to be true. In *The Future of an Illusion*, Freud maintains, on this basis, that illusions and delusions differ qualitatively. However, most cases are not clear-cut and, even if they were, it is not clear why that would imply a qualitative difference. This may be why in *Civilization and Its Discontents*, Freud allowed the distinction to lapse, describing theistic convictions as delusions outright.

*   *   *

Freud was unclear about precisely what his account of theism explains. There are therefore two ways to construe the explanation he advanced: a Darwinian way and a Feuerbachian way. The Darwinian way is agnostic on the question of how theism came into being; the Feuerbachian way is not. Because it is less ambitious, the Darwinian way is less easily undone by psychoanalytic theory's vulnerabilities. It is also more in line with what *The Future of an Illusion* delivers.

On a Darwinian reading, the position Freud developed in *The Future of an Illusion* does not explain the origin of theistic beliefs.[8] It is therefore compatible with the account that can be extrapolated out of *The Elementary Forms of Religious Life* or indeed with any view that allows for the possibility of nontheistic forms of religious ideation. What matters is just that theistic ideas become available. When they are, the mind gravitates towards them for the reasons Freud maintained. The analogy with the theory of evolution by natural selection is plain. For Darwin, variations in biological populations occur for reasons that evolutionary theory deems random—not because they are uncaused but because they fall outside the purview of the theory. Random variations are determined by natural laws like everything else in nature and are therefore explainable in principle; but they are not explained by natural selection. Natural selection explains what comes later; it explains how changes that came about for other reasons become more or less predominant in biological populations. The idea, in short, is that natural selection enhances "fitness," where traits are more or less fit according to how advantageous they are for the survival of particular populations in their respective environmental niches. The more conducive a variation is for survival, the more likely it is that organisms that have that trait will live long enough to reproduce. Variations that enhance fitness will therefore be passed on to succeeding generations. Therefore, in time, they will become prevalent.[9] But natural selection does not create fitness-enhancing properties; it works on what is there already. In much the same way, one could say that the unconscious processes that make theism appealing and resistant to extinction don't cause theistic ideas to come into being; they too only work with what is available to them for other reasons.

These processes emerge in the Oedipal phase of mental development. Therefore individuals' susceptibilities to theistic illusions are by-products of their struggles to resolve Oedipal conflicts; just as are individuals' susceptibilities to clinically diagnosable neuroses. Oedipal conflicts involve mental representations of the primordial family drama and therefore of its key protagonists, the mother and father. This is why Freud's account is susceptible to a Feuerbachian reading—according to which the God idea of the Abrahamic faiths, the Heavenly Father, is caused to come into being thanks to (unconscious) mental representations of the earthly father. Feuerbach's account of God was steeped in Hegelian metaphysics and post-Kantian philosophical anthropology. In a less portentous idiom—influenced, as many facets of our intellectual culture are, by Freudian psychology—one could say that God is a "projection" of ideas human beings have of themselves. This *naturalized* reformulation of Feuerbach's idea would explain theism's hold over the human mind on the grounds that the idea of God is inherent in our consciousness of ourselves, in our (unconscious) awareness of our humanity.

Freud's aim, again, was to develop a scientific account of the unconscious. No doubt, he believed that he succeeded, and that he therefore did naturalize insights implicit in the work of some of his less scientifically minded predecessors, including Feuerbach. But his explanations, though scientific in form and intent, are contentious, and the use he made of them was more suggestive than substantive. This diminishes the plausibility of a Feuerbachian reading of *The Future of an Illusion*. Freud never quite explained *how* human traits come to be represented in the idea of an Abrahamic God, and in the absence of a suitable account, there is no satisfactory explanation of where the idea of God comes from. One might therefore conclude that, on this key point, Freud's work bears on Feuerbach's only insofar as it vaguely suggests a way to recast Feuerbach's main contention—that man makes God, not vice versa—in a more congenial idiom.

Of course, if Freud was wrong about the stages of mental development and their connections to clinical phenomena—if there are no Oedipal conflicts or if their nature and resolutions differ substantially from what Freud maintained—then the Freudian explanation for theism's tenacity would have to be dismissed, whether it is construed in a Feuerbachian or a Darwinian way. However, for our purpose, it hardly matters whether his explanation is correct. What matters is how it or explanations relevantly like it impugn theism. Freud's account illustrates perspicaciously how reason-irrelevant causal explanations *can* make theism seem untenable, even if they don't refute its claims outright.

Freud explained theism's tenacity or, on a Feuerbachian reading, its tenacity plus its origin in the same way that he explained the genesis and sustenance of neuroses—conditions that are paradigmatically pathological. Thus, at a certain level of abstraction, theism and neuroses have common causes. This is not necessarily damning. But it is natural to find common features in phenomena that spring from the same source. Of course, there are differences. Theistic convictions are seldom disabling in the way that neuroses are. Quite the contrary: wherever there is social support for adhering to one or another Abrahamic faith, as there is nearly everywhere even to this day, there is seldom much to lose, and often much to gain, by being a believer. Seldom, if ever, do religious rituals or the beliefs they sustain cause as much unhappiness as diagnosable neuroses do; indeed, they often provide "consolation" and even joy. Nevertheless, it is fair to say that Freud's account of theism's tenacity—and perhaps also of its origin—suggests that the faith the Abrahamic religions promote has a pathological character, as well as a pathological etiology. It implies that the faithful suffer from a socially acceptable neurosis. The "opium of the people" may alleviate more pain than it causes. But it is still relevantly like a disease!

Freud's diagnosis is novel, but his appeal to healthfulness as a normative standard is not. From time immemorial, it has been taken for granted that health is good and illness bad. This conviction has been a bedrock assumption of all the healing arts for as long as they have been practiced. Since psycho-analysis is and always has been a branch of psychiatry, Freud's commitment to healthfulness is implicit in its basic orienta-tion. Psychoanalysis aims, as all medical practice does, at alle-viating and, where possible, curing illness; in other words, at restoring health. Because the Oedipal conflicts that are at the root of the illnesses psychoanalysis treats admit of no entirely satisfactory cure, unqualified mental health is an ideal that is all but impossible to realize. But it is an ideal that can be approximated, the more closely the better. It can be approxi-mated in cultures, too. A society that rids itself of theistic illu-sions is a healthier, saner society than one in the grip of faith.

*   *   *

In *Civilization and Its Discontents*, Freud responded to a criti-cism of *The Future of an Illusion* put forward by Romain Rol-land, a man he "much admired."[10] His rejoinder to Roland's criticism has implications for assessments of contemporary efforts by cognitive psychologists and others to investigate Abrahamic religiosity from a more securely scientific stand-point than Freud's. It is also relevant to assessments of defenses of theism that appeal to direct experience or to the testimony of others claiming to have had experiences that convey knowledge of the divine.

Rolland claimed that the origin of religious belief is an "oceanic feeling," a sense of oneness with a vastness so great that it fills those who experience it with awe. Freud never questioned the reality of experiences of this kind. Like

William James, he regarded the "varieties of religious experience," sincerely reported, as incontestable data.[11] What Freud questioned was their cognitive significance; their role in grounding theistic beliefs. Oceanic feelings are genuine from a subjective point of view, but they tell us nothing about the existence of a transcendent being outside our imaginations. The question they raise is not what information they convey, but why they seem to be informative at all.

To feel at one with something that is not oneself is to transgress the boundaries between the self and the other—boundaries forged in the earliest stages of maturation. The oceanic feeling therefore arises in consequence of breakdowns in mental structures that lie deeper in the unconscious than those arising out of Oedipal conflicts. In their origin and in their nature, they are of a piece with psychoses. As we have seen, Freud's account of theism, the one Rolland questioned, also appeals to pathological causes. But the mental structures Freud implicated are comparatively superficial. Their pathology is treatable; they can even be *talked through*. Oceanic feelings are a different matter. Fortunately, for most people, these feelings are fleeting and comparatively mild in intensity; they pass. There are, of course, significant and tragic exceptions; overt pathologies can and sometimes do present themselves in a religious guise. Then, like psychoses of no ostensible religious bearing, they can be profoundly painful and incapacitating. Presumably, the experiences Rolland had in mind were at the benign end of the continuum. But they are still enough like extreme forms of mental illness to warrant censure on grounds of morbidity. Like delusory reports of auditory, visual or tactile sensations made by persons in the throes of diagnosable psychoses or suffering more temporary psychotic episodes, oceanic feelings are of no use in detecting any reality outside the mind.

Similar states of mind can be drug induced for reasons that are only now becoming clear. Thanks to advances in the study of brain chemistry and in the larger field of neuro-science, we are on the threshold of a deeper, more biologically focused, understanding of oceanic feelings than was available in Freud's time. Perhaps some day too psychology will be able to explain why there are ostensibly normal people who are drawn to theistic convictions for reasons similar to Rolland's. Not everyone is susceptible to oceanic feelings; for better or worse, the "gift" is rare.

The experience Rolland named stands on the threshold of the mystical. Mystics believe that they apprehend the divine directly. If Freud was right, they do nothing of the sort. Mystical experiences result from collapses, usually temporary, of the boundaries between the self and the other. They are consequences of psychological malfunctions to which minds, some more than others, are prone. Phenomenologically, they can seem as real as anything could. But they are not *about* anything.

Can we nevertheless learn something about the world outside ourselves from mystical or near-mystical experiences? The answer, again, is *no*; these experiences tell us only about our own states of mind. The opposite view is widely held, of course, but there are at least two ways to rebut it. The first, Freud's way, is not available to persons skeptical of psycho-analysis, though something like it probably will become available to everyone in due course, as psychology and brain science advance. It is to establish explanations that account for mystical experiences, or pale approximations of them, in ways that undermine their cognitive pretensions. Were Freud's explanation of mysticism unassailable, the case would be closed. But his account is problematic; hence the appeal of the second way. It does not depend on any contentious psychological theory. However, it is more suggestive than conclusive. This second way just involves taking seriously two pertinent facts: that, as already noted, ostensibly revelatory experiences can be chemically induced; and that interpretations of experiences that claim to provide access to a transcendent reality are saturated with culturally relative ideations and affects that tarnish their claims to reveal the universal truths they purport to show.

The first of these facts speaks for itself. In principle, God could communicate with human beings directly, by causing them to have experiences of the kind that seem to establish his reality while, at the same time, subjectively similar—indeed, indistinguishable—experiences could be caused by self-induced or medically administered psychopharmacological interventions. But for anyone who keeps both possibilities in mind, the idea that mystics have direct knowledge of the divine would be as hard to accept as theism itself is for anyone who believes that God cements his hold over the human mind through a psychological mechanism that gives rise to pathological disorders. Mystical experiences are only states of mind. If, subjectively, they are qualitatively like states of mind that everyone agrees have no cognitive import, it would be implausible to conclude on this basis that they reveal anything about the world outside the mind.

Nevertheless, people are inclined to think that mystical experiences somehow do provide access to an otherwise inaccessible and "higher" reality. It is remarkable, however, that this reality almost always accords with the religious ideation of the ambient culture, and almost never involves ideas alien to it. The Virgin Mary appears to Catholics. Muslim and Jewish mystics have their own apparitional figures, angels mostly, and so do adherents of non-Abrahamic faiths. Is it not odd that divine beings should respect individual and cultural expectations so scrupulously! In drug-induced oceanic feelings, and in similar experiences of greater duration or intensity, interpretations are as varied as the people in whose minds they occur. Those who came of age in a secular environment or who have risen above the religious traditions into which they were born or who were born into religious traditions that, like Buddhism, are basically nontheistic, interpret mystical or quasimystical experiences in nontheistic, though "spiritual," ways. It is only people who have been socialized to identify spirituality with theism who find support for theism in mystical experiences. Of course, this observation, like all the others, does not strictly refute the interpretations mystics of a theistic bent provide. But by any standard less demanding than strict logical confutation, it does render them unworthy of serious consideration.

* * *

It has long been clear that there is no rationally defensible case *for* theism. As the case *against* it develops, the future of that illusion should grow dimmer. It would be foolish to expect that reason will triumph any time soon. That was one of Feuerbach's mistakes. But as theistic illusions come to seem more like delusions in Freud's sense, their allure is bound to diminish. Then a key part of the Young Hegelian project will have been achieved: humankind will be free from theism's yoke. This may not suffice to establish heaven on earth, but it will enable efforts to transform the real world conditions that make theistic illusions both necessary and possible; and to replace them with social and political institutions suitable for genuinely emancipated and enlightened women and men.

CHAPTER FOUR

BEYOND GOD AND EVIL

I t was Friedrich Nietzsche who famously proclaimed the death of God. He also wrote unkind things about Judaism and Jews—giving anti-Semites, including Nazis, reason to claim him as one of their own. He was even more hostile towards Christianity, especially its plebian versions, and to other aspects of German peasant culture. This is ironic in view of the enthusiasm with which German nationalists and their cothinkers on the European Right embraced his thought. In recent decades, Nietzsche has been praised and reviled for having anticipated forms of conceptual relativism that "postmodernists" would advance decades later. It will be instructive to comment briefly and in reverse order on these aspects of his thought before turning to what is directly germane to his indictment of faith in the modern era: his account of an *ethical* shortcoming believers exhibit. Though not in so many words, he, even more plainly than Freud, reproached believers for being in bad faith.

* * *

Because Nietzsche's formulations can suggest conceptual relativism, postmodernists see Nietzsche as an exponent of the views they champion and therefore as an opponent of the so-called "Enlightenment project." Yet, at its core, Nietzsche's case against the Abrahamic religions appealed, as much as Freud's or Durkheim's or Feuerbach's, to an imperative implicit in the defining Enlightenment principle: the injunction to face reality as an adult would—in Kant's words, to free oneself from "self-imposed nonage," or, as Kant also declared, "to dare to know."[1] However, Nietzsche made his case in a way that is sometimes confused and sometimes deliberately ironic. Careless readers or "theorists" with an agenda to promote are therefore easily misled.

Was he a conceptual relativist? The answer is not as straightforward as one might expect, and not just because, as the question is posed, it assumes that there is a fact of the matter; something conceptual relativism denies. The answer is complicated because there are several senses of relativism with which Nietzsche's views connect. A few definitions are therefore in order before taking on the question of Nietzsche's relativism.

Sentences that genuinely make assertions express *propositions*. Propositions are either true or false. This is the case whether or not their truth or falsity is known or even knowable. However, the truth-values of some propositions depend upon how their terms are related. When this is so, assertions about one or another of the terms involved are true or false *relative* to other terms in the proposition. This sort of relativism in no way embarrasses the claim that propositions are either true or false. Einstein's theory of (special) relativity is relativistic in this sense. According to that theory, space, time, and velocity are related to one another inasmuch as what is true or false of one or another of these phenomena depends on its relation to the others. This finding of Einstein's has had far-reaching implications. But the idea that claims about space, time, and velocity are any less true or false than they were thought to be in pre-Einsteinian times is not among them.

There are also philosophical theories that are relativistic. There are, for example, moral relativists who believe that the truth or falsity of claims about what morality requires—that killing is wrong or that one ought to help others—depend on their relation to other pertinent facts: for example, the identities of the agents or prevailing cultural norms. So conceived, moral relativism does not imply that claims about killing or helping others lack truth values; only that their truth or falsity is relative to something beyond just the fact of agency itself. There are also *noncognitivist* metaethical theories, theories about ethics, that deny that moral judgments have truth-values. On this view, "killing is wrong" or "helping others is right" merely express positive or negative views about killing or helping others, and perhaps also efforts to persuade others to agree. All noncognitivist theories are relativist; they all hold that moral attitudes are relative to the persons whose attitudes they are. But moral relativism can and usually is formulated in ways that reject noncognitivism. To hold that claims about the rightness or wrongness of killing or helping others are, say, agent-relative does not, on the usual understanding, imply that assessments of particular instances of killing or helping are neither true nor false.

Nietzsche was committed to positions in moral theory

that could plausibly be described as relativist in a cognitivist sense. He thought that judgments of right and wrong depend on who the agents are and whom their actions affect. However, his purchase on that idea was so extreme that, by his own lights and on plausible readings of his views, it exceeded the boundaries of moral theory altogether. To the extent this is so, Nietzsche was not, strictly speaking, a *moral* relativist. He was a *critic* of morality—from a non- or extramoral, but still ethical, point of view.

The relativism of postmodernists who see Nietzsche as a precursor is epitomized in the slogan attributed by Plato to the ancient Greek philosopher Protagoras—that "of all things man is the measure, of the being of things that are and of the not being of things that are not." This saying implies that there is no objective point of view; no account of what is the case that is independent of particular *human* vantage points. Things *seem* one way or another to particular observers, but there is no further fact of the matter and therefore no way things *really* are. There is a sense in which it is consistent with this contention that propositions are true or false for particular persons. But they cannot be objectively true or false— true or false from all vantage points. This is tantamount to saying that there are no truths (or falsehoods) at all; only observer-relative "seemings."

When postmodernists ascribe this position to Nietzsche, they draw on two related themes in his work: his account of God's death and its implications for truth, and his claims for the constitutive role and universality of "the will to power." Some discussion of these matters will follow in due course.

For now, I would just point out that a global relativism of the Protagorean kind is self-refuting. If there are no objective truths, then it is neither true nor false that relativism is true. This rebuttal of all-encompassing relativism has been in circulation since ancient times. But, no matter how often Protagorean relativism is refuted, the doctrine refuses to remain forever dead. Thus it has been suggested lately that relativism with respect to everything can be maintained by adopting an "ironic" as opposed to a "metaphysical" point of view.[2] Then, supposedly, one can make assertions without meaning what one says, and without these assertions having truth-values. When this view is attributed to Nietzsche or when he is enlisted in its support, it follows that, whatever he may have thought, he was not committed to doctrines at all. But, as we will see, Nietzsche plainly did believe in the truth of several "metaphysical" positions, and he was not wrong to do so. Nietzsche was a master ironist, to be sure, but not in a way that implies Protagorean relativism.

*　　*　　*

Nowhere is the ironic side of Nietzsche's thought more evident than in his account of his own philosophical mission. Hegelian philosophy and its positivist rival shaped the intellectual culture Nietzsche encountered. It was therefore into this framework that he intervened. As we have seen, both Hegel and the positivists advanced notions of triadic development. For Hegel, an endogenous dynamic made this so: "theses" develop "antitheses" which are then joined together into a "synthesis" or higher unity. For Comte and his successors in the positivist tradition, the idea that history can be divided into three epochal stages—pretheistic, theistic, and post-theistic (scientific, secular)—was descriptive only; these are categories for organizing empirical data, and nothing more. This is enough, however, for positivists to ascribe a structure and directionality to human history, just as Hegelians do. According to postmodernists, Nietzsche rejected Hegelian *and* positivist positions, along with "master-narratives" generally, setting in motion the deconstruction of them all by revealing how they operate rhetorically either to facilitate domination or to articulate the resentment of those who are dominated. In their view, it was to this end that he concocted a master-narrative of his own, with its own triadic structure.

Nietzsche equivocated about exactly what the "thesis" was: sometimes it was the world of Greco-Roman antiquity, sometimes it was primitive "heroic" culture. Thus, to the delight of German nationalists, Nietzsche glorified ancient Germanic barbarism, notwithstanding his admiration for Greek and Roman civilization. The identity of the "antithesis" was clearer: it was Christian civilization, the world historical heir of the Judaic "negation" of heroic culture. In Nietzsche's view, morality was a Jewish invention, taken over by Christianity—largely, though not entirely, to the detriment of what is estimable in the ways of life it negated. Nietzsche then contended that these forms of civilization, the Greco-Roman (or, alternatively, the heroic) and the moral, would eventually coexist in a higher unity. The new order will be a fitting abode for the "superman" or *übermensch*, he who overcomes the "human all too human" by incorporating what is worth retaining in ancient and Christian civilizations into a new "synthesis."[3] To hasten his coming, the philosopher's task is to "negate" the negation by overturning doctrines that oppose the heroic ethos—exposing the untenability and, wherever possible, the contradictory implications of morality's core assumptions.

Morality was targeted because it subsumes all human beings under the same "laws," without regard to the differences—in nobility and baseness—that were central to the ethical thought of other civilizations. But morality is not the only target. The real enemy is objectivity itself—the "God's eye view" that Spinoza called "the aspect of eternity." In its place, Nietzsche would introduce or rather reinstate not global relativism but *perspectivism*; the idea that there are only particular perspectives of different, and differentially meritorious, knowers and doers. In their own ways, both Jerusalem and Athens, as Nietzsche conceived them, aspired to a God's eye view, though only Jerusalem unequivocally carried this aspiration into the ethical realm. Epistemological and ethical perspectivism are relativistic positions inasmuch as they claim that what one can know and what one ought to do depend on one's circumstances and on who one is and, in ethical matters, upon whom one is acting.

Carried to the extreme, a thoroughgoing perspectivism threatens to exceed the horizons of relativisms that maintain that there are facts of the matter, passing over into what Nietzsche sometimes called *nihilism*. "Nihilism" was a political term that Nietzsche appropriated and used in apolitical ways. Most often, he used it to describe his own philosophical

program, a project appropriate for a world coming to terms
with the death of God. In these circumstances, the principal
philosophical task is to expedite the demise of ways of
thinking that depend on the God idea or, what seems to have
come to the same thing for him, that aspire to a God's eye
view—in other words, to demolish philosophy itself as it
existed up to his day. This was why Nietzsche proclaimed that
he "philosophized with a hammer," and why he called himself
and those who would join him *nihilists*.[4] Like political nihilists,
who seek to level or annihilate regimes they oppose, the better
to construct something radically new, the philosophical
nihilist is a harbinger of new ways of thinking and acting and
therefore of a new form of civilization.

Postmodernists claim that Nietzsche's nihilism took aim
at truth itself. However, this cannot be, and not just because
Nietzsche advanced claims that he showed every sign of
believing. His doctrine of the will to power, which is indispensable for recasting his theoretical pronouncements as
ironic gestures made for rhetorical effect, undoes any possible
Protagorean relativist construal of his view. For even if we do
not take Nietzsche's position at its word, but instead view it,
along with everything else, as an expression of itself, of the
will to power, it must still be true—metaphysically, not just
ironically—that there is a will to power. This is yet another
example of the general problem Protagorean or global relativism confronts; it is self-refuting. Even if there is no objective (nonperspectival) truth about, say, whether what I see
before me is green, since I cannot be wrong that it seems
green to me, it is true that I see green. Even if all metaphys-

ical positions are expressions of the will to power, it is true that the will to power is real. Whatever global relativists may think, we cannot dispense with truth altogether. Nietzsche understood this full well.

The nihilism that postmodernists credit Nietzsche with discovering must not be confused with more moderate relativist and perspectival positions. And we should be especially wary, where God is concerned, of identifying professions of relativism with the genuine article. Indeed, it is hard to imagine what relativism with respect to God's existence might mean, though it is often said that "God exists" for some people but not for others. Appearance to the contrary, this is not a genuinely relativist contention but a misleading way of saying that some people, but not others, believe that "God exists." However, there is an unlikely but not entirely implausible way to deny that "God exists" is true or false—namely, by claiming that there is no proposition corresponding to the assertion. In the 1920s and for several decades thereafter, the logical positivists held a view of this sort. These intellectual descendants of Comte, Durkheim's intellectual cousins, subscribed to a theory of meaning, *verificationism*, according to which sentences that appear to assert propositions are meaningful if and only if what they claim can in principle be verified empirically. "God exists" fails to meet this standard; so does "God does not exist." Therefore, according to verificationists, these assertions are meaningless; they no more succeed in asserting propositions than do arbitrary strings of nonsense syllables. The difference is that "God exists" is not nonsense on its face, the way that, say, "blah blah blah" is. In the former case, we are misled by language into thinking that we are asserting something; in the latter, we are not. But in neither case are we asserting anything at all. If "God exists" is like "blah blah blah" in this respect, it would be neither true nor false, except in the trivial sense that a declarative sentence that fails to assert a true proposition is false. Then theism (or deism) would not be true or false either; and atheism would be similarly meaningless or else true only in the sense that its negation is not.

The Young Hegelians were atheists, not nihilists; in their view, "God exists" is meaningful but false. Nevertheless, logical positivism and Young Hegelianism are alike in one important respect: they are both irreligious in their practical effects. The logical positivists believed that right-thinking people would disabuse themselves of nonsense, and that when they do, they would *ipso facto* free themselves from the doctrines, practices, and institutions nonsensical beliefs sustain. The implications for religion are obvious. However, unlike the Young Hegelians for whom Christianity was Topic A, the logical positivists exhibited a healthy disinterest in religious matters. Nevertheless their (largely) implicit diagnosis of theism (or deism) complements Feuerbach's. Taking a logical positivist understanding of "God exists" to heart should produce as profound a transformation of consciousness as anything Feuerbach envisioned. Seeing theism as nonsensical might not lead people to substitute faith in man for faith in God, but it would provide a path for getting beyond faith altogether.

Logical positivism also provides a clearer model than can be found in Nietzsche's writings for Nietzsche's admonition to philosophize "with a hammer." However, before hastening to join the logical positivists to Nietzsche or to enlist logical positivism in the struggle against bad faith, we should note that the logical positivists' theory of meaning is untenable. Verificationism, like Protagorean relativism, fails to satisfy its own standard; it is therefore self-defeating. For this and other reasons, it has passed into the historical memory of analytical philosophers and behavioral scientists. Nevertheless, there is a lesson to be drawn from the unsuccessful efforts of the logical positivists' assault on traditional metaphysics. It is that nihilism with respect to "God exists" is conceivable. Less radical versions of relativism with respect to God's existence fail even that test. To what, after all, could the existence of a supreme being of the kind deists and therefore theists think real be relative?

Again, Nietzsche was not a genuine nihilist with respect to faith or the larger epistemological issues he associated with it. He was an atheist in the Enlightenment tradition. And neither was he a nihilist with respect to ethics; he was a critic of morality or, one might say, an amoralist.

*   *   *

An *ethic* is a guide to what persons ought to do or how they should assess what they or others do. *Morality* is a kind of ethic—one that bases deliberations and assessments on universal principles or "laws." Inasmuch as the principles moral theorists advance apply to all agents equally, morality assumes a point of view that accords no special weight to any particular perspective, including one's own. How matters stand with respect to some agents but not others, including oneself, is irrelevant; what matters is agency in general. A philosophically unelaborated expression of this idea is implicit in the New Testament's Golden Rule: "do unto others, as you would have others do unto you." This dictum seems to command that, in deliberating about what to do, factors that distinguish oneself from others should not be taken into account; that only commonalities should. But, ultimately, the only thing that all moral agents have in common is agency itself. It was on this basis that Kant transformed the Golden Rule into a *categorical* (unconditional) *imperative* that dictates that, where moral considerations apply, agents should act on "maxims" (principles of action) that they can coherently will to apply to moral agents as such.[5] So understood, moral theory was unknown to the ancient Greeks or to ethicists in Asian cultures or to the "heroic" ancestors of modern Germans.

Nietzsche was probably right in holding that the moral point of view was an invention of ancient Israel in the Prophetic age. He was right too in maintaining that, in the centuries that followed, the moral point of view came increasingly to shape Jewish and Christian ethics—and, presumably, the ethical thought of Islamic cultures. However, despite its origins, moral theory has a fundamentally secular character. Its rationale follows not from any divine commandment, but from the need, shared by all members of putatively moral communities, to justify their actions to themselves and to each other on a basis of equal consideration and respect. This is why no moral theorist of any standing in the modern era has maintained that morality stands or falls with God. It is telling

too that, from the time Kant's account of the nature of
morality began to register in philosophical circles, some religious thinkers—Søren Kierkegaard, for example—
distinguished morality from faith. Nevertheless, as Nietzsche
discerned, there is a sense in which the idea of God, or rather
of a God's eye view, is central to moral thought. Morality supposes that notions of right and wrong and good and bad are
objective, that the principles moral agents employ in deliberating about what to do are equally binding on agents as such.
This is the "rational kernel," as Marx would say, implicit in
Nietzsche's insistence that morality cannot withstand God's
demise. But Nietzsche was wrong to suggest that the urge to
attain a God's eye cannot survive the death of God. He was
wrong to tie morality to God in the way that he did. Nevertheless, his mistake is instructive.

* * *

In proclaiming the death of God, Nietzsche's point was obviously not that an omnipotent, omniscient, perfectly good
being had passed away, as all living organisms must. His aim
instead was to announce the passing of an epochal stage of
human history—one that he identified with a structure of
thought based upon the aspiration to attain a God's eye view.
That Nietzsche would periodize epochal historical structures
in an idealist fashion is ironic inasmuch as he seems simultaneously to appropriate Hegel's idealist philosophy of history
while rejecting the notions of truth and falsity upon which it
was based. But Nietzsche's periodization of history into struc-

tures defined by modes of thought was not just an ironic gesture. For reasons that have mainly to do with his doctrine of the will to power, he really did believe that the unmediated perspectivism that he thought he found in pre-Christian thinking could be joined with advances made during the Christian era into a new and higher unity. This new order would have an ethical dimension. But its implications, as Nietzsche foresaw, are as much theoretical as practical; science probably, and philosophy certainly, would be radically transformed.

There is a sense in which, for Nietzsche as for Hegel, what makes this next stage possible and also necessary are developments internal to the preceding period. But Nietzsche was closer to the positivists than to the Hegelians in a key respect: he rejected any notion of an immanent dynamic propelling history forward towards its end. There is not even an inexorable natural sequencing of the kind Durkheim described. For Nietzsche, the future is open—the "overcoming" of the old order that he prophesied is a possibility only, not an historical tendency, much less a historical inevitability.[6] In acknowledging the radical contingency of the future, the nature and complexity of his assessment of the so-called Enlightenment project, and his unambivalent commitment to the values that sustained it, come into focus.

It was the unfolding of an intellectual dynamic launched under the aegis of Enlightenment ideals that brought about God's demise. According to the standards enlightened thinkers insist upon, deism and therefore theism fail to pass muster. For Nietzsche, this conclusion is too obvious to war-

136

rant further attention, just as it was for Feuerbach, Durkheim, and Freud. The question for him, as for the others, was not whether belief in God is defensible, plainly it is not, but what follows from its indefensibility—in a world that has so far only begun to assimilate the news of his death. Notwithstanding the views of some of Nietzsche's admirers, what does not follow is that enlightened thinking must give way to a global conceptual relativism. Enlightened thinking made God's death inevitable, it assures that God stays dead in the face of all that makes the opium of the people appealing, and it provides the only possible basis for contemplating what can and should follow in the post-theistic period ahead.

* * *

Nietzsche claimed that the assumption of a God's eye view is one way among others that an omnipresent will to power is expressed. But it is unclear what he thought a will to power is. Though it plainly has a psychological dimension, he did not think of it as a psychological drive, like libido was for Freud. For one thing, it is everywhere; not just in the mind. For another, Nietzsche depicted the will to power in a way that eludes empirical corroboration or disconfirmation.

Nietzsche was a psychologist of the first order, but his insights were intuitive; no underlying psychological theory sustained them, as in the case of Freud. Like Arthur Schopenhauer, the philosopher whom Nietzsche called his "educator," Nietzsche regarded the will, volition, not mind, as the inner content and driving force of the world; prior to thought and

therefore to knowledge and, in a sense, even to being itself.
Exactly what he or Schopenhauer meant by this is obscure. But
it is clear that Nietzsche's and Schopenhauer's contentions are
as insusceptible to naturalistic reconstructions as was Feuerbach's account of essential humanity. Nietzsche produced
nothing analogous to the theories that Freud and his followers
concocted. Freud's account of the libido's career—of its subli-
mation, refinement, and expression—and his "discovery" of
the death instinct, have no counterpart in Nietzsche's writings.
This is why Freud's views are more vulnerable to refutation,
but also why they are more explanatory. Freud's foremost aim
was to discover how the mind—or rather, its unconscious
part—functions, and to put his findings to work in curing
mental illnesses. There is no place in such a project for a metaphysical principle that is empirically empty and therefore
explanatorily inert. Nevertheless, Nietzsche's position was in
one respect more penetrating than Freud's. Nietzsche discovered a normative dimension to healthfulness that most clini-
cians fail to see, and that even Freud hardly grasped.

* * *

There are reasons why health matters that are universally
acknowledged. Illness, including mental illness, is typically
accompanied by pain—and pain is everywhere deemed bad.
Health is therefore valued because it alleviates suffering. Illnesses also impede human functioning. This, too, is bad. But
there are, in addition, normative dimensions to the standard of
healthfulness that Nietzsche discerned that go beyond these

understandings by connecting with a strain of ethical thought based upon the "virtue ethics" of Greek antiquity.

The preeminent philosopher of virtue ethics was Aristotle.[7] On his view, to become what one is, to self-actualize, is intrinsically, not just instrumentally, good. Thus it is good in itself that all things, including human beings, actualize their capacities; that they become all that they can be. This is the core idea conveyed in his writings on particular virtues. As Aristotle's teacher, Plato, put it, the virtue of a thing is that which permits it to perform its function well; thus the virtue of a knife is sharpness. The virtue of a person is to behave in ways that enhance human excellence. Aristotle's account of the virtues is therefore joined conceptually with a theory of what is appropriate for particular persons in particular circumstances. Virtuous persons are disposed to act in accord with the "mean" between excessive and deficient displays of relevant behaviors. Particular virtues are general names for dispositions to act appropriately in one or another domain. Vices are names of inappropriate extremes. Nietzsche joined this Aristotelian idea to prevailing notions of sickness and health—claiming that there are ways of being unhealthy that involve a failure properly to self-actualize and therefore to develop dispositions to act in appropriate ways.

Ever the clinician, Freud was committed to healthfulness for the usual reasons. He never blamed the ill for their afflictions in the way Aristotle—and Nietzsche—would hold individuals accountable for lapses of virtue. But there is nevertheless a sense in which Freudian theory assumes the normative perspective Nietzsche adopted. On Freud's account, there are healthy and unhealthy ways for libido to become manifest. A goal of psychoanalytic therapy is to make healthy manifestations prevail. A similar goal motivated Freud's accounts of cultural phenomena—including religion. He sought to promote the "health" of civilizations.

Similarly, for Nietzsche, healthfulness—construed not in the literal, clinical sense, but in accord with his metaphysical convictions—was a preeminent ideal.[8] This passage, from *The Gay Science*, illustrates this point:

> *Health of the soul.*—The popular medical formulation of morality that goes back to Ariston of Chios, "virtue is the health of the soul," would have to be changed to become useful, at least to read: "*your* virtue is the health of *your* soul." For there is no health as such, and all attempts to define a thing that way have been wretched failures. Even the determination of what is healthy for your *body* depends on your goal, your horizon, your energies, your impulses, your errors, and above all on the ideals and phantasms of your soul. Thus there are innumerable healths of the body; and the more we allow the unique and incomparable to raise its head again, the more we abjure the dogma of "the equality of men," the more must the concept of a *normal* health, along with a normal diet, and the normal course of an illness, be abandoned by medical men. Only then would the time have come to reflect on the health and illness of the *soul*, and to find the peculiar virtue of each man in the health of his soul. In one person, of course, this health could look like its opposite in another person....

What is remarkable is how Nietzsche's particularized the standard. Because the received understanding of healthfulness suffers from the taint of objectivity—or, what comes to the same thing for Nietzsche, because it has been shaped by ways of thinking that are incognizant of God's death—it must be reconstructed to become truly useful. It must be perspectivized in a way that accommodates differences among persons; differences that are of evaluative, not just empirical (or clinical), significance.

Whether or not this is yet another example of Nietzschean perspectivism run amok, it does point to a deeper understanding of the evaluative principle Freud had in mind. What lies at the heart of Nietzsche's case against morality and its counterparts in the domain of theoretical reason has a dimension that terms like "healthy" and "ill" only suggest. Nietzsche never named the standard he endorsed, but decades later, existentialists in Germany and France, drawing on his work, called it *authenticity*—their point, and Nietzsche's, being that it is intrinsically good to be what one truly is; in other words, to be *honest* not just in what one says or does but, so to speak, in one's very being.

A commitment to authenticity is implicit in Nietzsche's most sustained attack on morality, *The Genealogy of Morals*, where he laments the transformation of the good/bad ethics of pre-Christian times into an ethic of good and evil.[9] The good/bad dichotomy is more aesthetic than moral; though, unlike specifically aesthetic notions, it is applicable to persons and deeds, not just works of art or raw nature. The idea is that persons, moved by a will to power, should express their will to the utmost limits of their intrinsic worth—by fashioning their lives according to their own rules and in light of their own purposes. Kant had distinguished aesthetic from moral value. In his canonical formulation, the aesthetic realm is governed by organizational principles specific to particular objects, while the moral order is comprised of universally applicable laws.[10] Nietzsche turned Kant's distinction on its head. To live well, he maintained, is not to subordinate one's will to universally applicable principles, moral laws, but instead to fashion ways of acting that are true to one's nature—to live as if one were a character in a work of art one creates for oneself. This thought is elaborated in another passage from *The Gay Science*:

> *One thing is needful.*—To "give style" to one's character—a great and rare art. It is practiced by those who survey all the strengths and weaknesses of their nature and then fit them into an artistic plan until every one of them appears as art and reason and even weaknesses delight the eye. Here a large mass of second nature has been added; there a piece of original nature has been removed—both times through long practice and daily work at it. Here the ugly that could not be removed is concealed; there it is reinterpreted and made sublime. Much that is vague and resisted shaping has been saved and exploited for distant views; it is meant to beckon toward the far and immeasurable. In the end, when the work is finished, it becomes evident how the constraint of a single taste governed and formed everything large and small. Whether this taste was good or bad is less important than one might suppose, if only it was a single taste!
>
> It will be the strong and domineering natures that

enjoy their finest gaiety in such constraint and perfection under a law of their own; the passion of their tremendous will relents in the face of all stylized nature, of all conquered and serving nature. Even when they have to build palaces and design gardens they demur at giving nature freedom.

Conversely, it is the weak characters without power over themselves that *hate* the constraint of style. They feel that if the bitter and evil constraint were imposed upon them they would be demeaned; they become slaves as soon as they serve; they hate to serve....[11]

Morality is inimical to this objective because it obliterates differences. This is why, in Nietzsche's view, the deepest problem with morality is its inauthenticity. Where morality reigns, all agents deliberate from the same vantage point. But this defining feature of the moral point of view ignores particularities that are supremely important for an ethic of authenticity—especially gradations of merit, of (nonmoral) goodness. The moral point of view levels these ethically relevant differences—bringing the top *down* and the bottom *up*, permitting the weak, the less powerful, to achieve, by indirection, a kind of equality with, if not quite mastery over, those whom nature has made their superiors.

Nietzsche called Christianity's imposition of morality "a slave revolt."[12] His terminology has an Aristotelian and also a Hegelian resonance. For Aristotle, the authority masters exercise over slaves is in the natural order of things. Because slaves are slaves by nature, their subordination is justified. This is why it would be wrong for masters and slaves to be subject to the same laws. Needless to say, Aristotle's views on slavery are anachronistic. Despite this, or perhaps because of it, Nietzsche endorsed them, though without quite acknowledging doing so. In this way, he drew attention to a central tenet of his case against morality: his insistence, in contravention of the moral point of view, on the pertinence of agent-specificity.

Hegel too made much of the relation between master and slave, not because he defended slavery as an institution, but because he saw the dialectical interdependence of these categories as crucial to his main concern: the coming into self-consciousness of mind itself.[13] The master conceives himself qua master through the mind of the slave and vice versa. Some twentieth-century Marxists, intellectual descendants of Feuerbach, discovered emancipatory implications in Hegel's account, not least because he accorded preeminent importance in this dialectical engagement to the slave, the occupant of the subordinate position. Characteristically, Nietzsche turned Hegel's analysis on its head: maintaining, in Hegelian (dialectical) fashion, that morality represents an inversion of the ideal relation between masters and slaves. The God's eye view that morality imposes makes those who are slaves by nature the official equals and often the *de facto* masters of those who by nature ought to exercise authority over them. It enables the weak to do what they, along with everything else in the universe, are driven to do—to exercise power. But the weak cannot do so directly. They can only prevail in an inherently dishonest and indirect way—by establishing and then imposing the moral point of view.

The triumph of morality, of an ethic of good and evil over

an ethic of good and bad, had important psychological consequences: it transformed shame into guilt. According to Nietzsche, a shame/honor ethic was the norm before the triumph of morality. Then, under Christianity's aegis, shame gave way to bad conscience (guilt) and honor to guiltlessness. Nietzsche had nothing to say about how this transformation comes about at a psychological level. But he was acutely aware of the cultural importance of the transformation he described. Wherever shame gives way to guilt, it is because the (naturally) mighty have internalized rules that place them, along with the (naturally) weak, under the same constraints. This transformation marks an epochal change in human history, and a major advance for inauthenticity. It marks the triumph of sickness over health, of darkness over light. Nietzsche repeatedly invoked these metaphors and others of a similar character in describing morality. His aim in doing so was to advance the nihilistic project—to hasten the negation of the negation by conveying the idea that morality, seen aright, hardly warrants "reverence," as Kant maintained, but the opposite; that it is repellent in the way that unhealthy circumstances and conditions are.

The Genealogy of Morals contains many passages that identify morality with sickness. Its entire second part, on guilt and bad conscience, derides the character of the internally generated repression that Freud would later cast in a naturalistic framework and describe in a clinically detached manner. The passage, excerpted below, from the first part of *The Genealogy of Morals,* conveys the tenor of Nietzsche's disdain:

Would anyone like to take a look into the secret of how ideals are made on earth? Who has the courage?—Very well! Here is a point we can see through into this dark workshop. But wait a moment or two, Mr. Rash and Curious: your eyes must first get used to this false iridescent light.—All right! Now speak! What is going on down there? Say what you see....

—"I see nothing, but I hear the more. There is a soft, wary, malignant muttering and whispering coming from all the corners and nooks. It seems to me one is lying; a saccharine sweetness clings to every sound. Weakness is being lied into something *meritorious*....

—"and impotence which does not requite into 'goodness of heart'; anxious lowliness into 'humility'; subjection to those one hates into 'obedience.'... The inoffensiveness of the weak man, even the cowardice of which he has so much, his lingering at the door, his being ineluctably compelled to wait, here acquire flattering names, such as 'patience,' and are even called virtue itself; his inability for revenge is called unwillingness to revenge, perhaps even forgiveness ('for they know not what they do—we alone know what they do')...."[14]

In short, morality reeks of disease, and whoever is able to appreciate that this is so cannot help but be repelled. No germ causes this disease. It is caused by a lie—an existential lie, as it were, a misrepresentation of the true nature of things. But, of course, this is a lie only in a manner of speaking. Full-fledged lies presume intentionality, and it is far from clear, even to Nietzsche, that, for all their guile, the perpetrators of morality's epochal assault on the mighty were aware of what they were doing. They were in the grip of a profound error, one that led them, as much as their victims, astray. Morality is based on deceit. It is an expression of bad faith, even according to Sartre's narrowly focused purchase on the idea.

A more authentic expression of the will to power would be cognizant of differences among people. To restore this sensibility—not by regressing to what was superseded with the death of the gods Christianity vanquished, but by incorporating that thesis and its negation (antithesis) into a higher unity in the aftermath of the Christian God's death—is to exchange darkness for light or, in a metaphorically equivalent sense, illness for health. Nietzsche used these descriptions interchangeably. This was rhetorically appropriate. The sun is a force for healing; its light cleanses. Bringing light upon the God's eye view is similarly salutary. An indispensable step in that direction is casting the light of reason upon God himself.

Nietzsche faulted the Jews for making Christianity possible and therefore, indirectly, for spreading monotheism—and the God's eye view along with it. He also praised the Jews for this because monumental villainy is itself an expression of greatness and is therefore, by Nietzsche's lights, deserving of esteem. For Christianity, he had fewer compliments. Popularizing what the Jews had invented was not its only sin. Authentic life affirmation consists in the direct expression of the will to power. Christianity, however, is life-negating. It promotes asceticism.[15] This too is (metaphorically) an illness. It is also the foundation of our form of civilization—something the world will be better off for overcoming.

Nietzsche's disdain for democratic politics and for egali-

tarian aspirations, including those for equality between men
and women, follow accordingly, inasmuch as democracy and
egalitarianism are, in Nietzsche's view, collective expressions
of the same, essentially Jewish and therefore Christian, ideal.
For democrats and egalitarians of all stamps, "all men [*sic*] are
created equal." Nietzsche insisted otherwise. Whether his
animus was sincere or only a rhetorical posture is immaterial.
What matters is his conviction that the first order of business
for philosophers today is to submit notions of equality in all
their guises to the nihilists' hammer.

*   *   *

Morality, in Nietzsche's view, is a trick foisted on masters by
slaves. In his Young Hegelian period and implicitly thereafter,
Marx defended a contrary position, reflecting a diametrically
opposed political orientation. Marx faulted morality because its
defining principle, agent neutrality, is a trick foisted on slaves by
their masters; because by taking no account of the determinative reality of class divisions and class struggle, it reinforces the
domination of subaltern classes. Nietzsche was concerned with
morality's political consequences too, though from a perspective friendly to class domination; he opposed morality from the
Right. However, he was more concerned with morality's implications for individual ethics than with its social and economic
effects. Marx was not; he did not dispute morality per se.
Indeed, the communism he envisioned, where class divisions
are overcome, would be a genuine moral order, a Kantian
"republic of ends." Marx's complaint against morality was only

that, this side of communism, universality is an unrealizable ideal. Inasmuch as the public institutions of the bourgeois state purport to be based on that ideal, on principles of universal Right (*Recht*), they function in just the opposite of the way moral theory supposes; instead of realizing freedom, they impede it— to the detriment of workers and other oppressed persons. Thus Nietzsche's case against morality, though less focused on politics, was more radical than Marx's; Nietzsche faulted the idea itself, not just its real-world applications.

For both thinkers, the ideas that define moral theory operate *ideologically*. Marx and Marxists after him made much of the idea underlying this contention, showing how in general ideas serve the interests of particular social groups. Their conception of ideology has spilled over into the mainstream culture. Nietzsche never used the word but he unwittingly absorbed the idea or else arrived at a similar understanding independently. In either case, it is fair to say that morality functions as an even more potent ideological construct for Nietzsche than for Marx because, in Nietzsche's view, it helps reproduce an entire civilization, not just an economic or political regime. Morality is the means by which slaves subdue and then dominate their masters. In doing so, it reproduces a system reeking of inauthenticity, in which, as Jesus said, "the meek . . . inherit the earth."[16]

*   *   *

Like Aristotle, Nietzsche was a *perfectionist*; he believed that the realization of potentialities, the "perfection" of individual excellence, is not just instrumentally good—say, for enhancing overall well-being—but that it is intrinsically good and therefore ought to be pursued regardless of its consequences. Like Aristotle, perhaps even more so, Nietzsche believed that potentialities are distributed unequally across human beings. But Nietzsche's position and Aristotle's were not quite the same. Once his views on slavery and related matters (including the role of women) are discarded as historical anachronisms, Aristotle's perfectionism can be, and often is, enlisted in the service of a democratic ethic that aims at the realization of *all* human potentialities, regardless of whose they are. Nietzsche's perfectionism resists a similar democratization because it is embedded in a historical narrative that precludes the possibility. On Nietzsche's account, the good society is not one in which all men and women realize their potentialities as much as their respective abilities and circumstances allow; it is one in which entire populations are mobilized to help the most meritorious realize *their* potentialities. Nietzsche thought that, for now and the foreseeable future, the best political regimes are those that prepare the way for the supermen (*Übermenschen*) who will emerge in the civilization that will arise in the aftermath of God's death. This is why his position cannot be sanitized in ways that render it inoffensive. It permits, indeed demands, that the many be sacrificed for the few.

* * *

Nietzsche was deceived by metaphor—his own and those of others. Thus he wrongly believed that a God's eye view presupposes a living God. But objectivity is a God's eye view only in a manner of speaking. God and a God's eye view are not connected in the way Nietzsche supposed.

To be sure, the idea that objectivity depends on God has a venerable philosophical pedigree. As noted, Descartes thought that the new sciences of nature would whither under skeptical attack unless there are unassailable reasons to believe that an omnipotent, omniscient, and *perfectly truthful* being guarantees their veracity. He then argued, to his own satisfaction, that such a guarantee is forthcoming. What the new sciences sought to do was to discover *objective* truths; to account for how things are, not from any particular vantage point, but from all possible vantage points or, what comes to the same thing, from nowhere specifically—how they are under what Spinoza called "the aspect of eternity." In treating objectivity among the casualties that follow from God's death, Nietzsche was therefore less original than might appear. But, in the time between the seventeenth century, when Descartes and Spinoza wrote, and the end of the nineteenth century, when Nietzsche did, and more so since, it has become clear that Descartes's position and Spinoza's, insofar as they bear on conceptions of objectivity, can be disentangled from their theistic (or, in Spinoza's case, pantheistic) commitments, and therefore that *their* accounts of the relation between God and objectivity are, in the final analysis, metaphorical too, whether they realized it or not.

It is clearer now than it used to be that objectivity is a humanly realizable objective that does not require guarantees, divinely based or otherwise; and that how things would appear to a perfect being, insofar as that idea makes sense, and how they objectively are, need not coincide. The first of these claims is beyond dispute: science trades in results that are reproducible and therefore confirmable from any and all vantage points. This is all objectivity need mean. Additional demands for guarantees are of no practical consequence.[17] Objective knowledge *works* in the sense that it provides bases for transforming nature to accord with human desires and needs. Notwithstanding the efforts of Descartes and his successors to defeat skepticism with respect to empirical knowledge, it has become clear that usefulness is all the evidence of objective truth that anyone could want.[18] Perhaps nature, the world science discovers, is all there is. Or, perhaps there is a reality beyond the one science apprehends that human beings can acknowledge but not know, as Kant maintained, or know extrascientifically, perhaps through the application of dialectical methods, as Hegel endeavored to show. This "noumenal" order is a better candidate than scientific knowledge for how things are "under the aspect of eternity." But there is still no reason to identify it with how, if God existed, things would appear to him.

We have no idea what a perfect being would know. Theists believe that, in addition to being all-powerful and perfectly good, God is omniscient; that he knows everything. But this does not imply that God knows everything from every possible (or actual) perspective. That would be tantamount to denying that there is a (unique) God's eye view. It would collapse the distinction between objective and subjective knowledge, making it impossible to say how things *really* are. This is why the theist (and deist) hold instead that God knows everything from his own perspective. But one need hardly have Feuerbach's powers of discernment to see that the properties theists (and deists) impute to God—omnipotence (because it involves agency) and perfect goodness (because it involves value)—have irreducibly anthropomorphic colorations; that God is like us, only (infinitely) more so. *Knowing* too is an eminently human achievement involving, among other things, belief and justification in addition to truth. Why should we think that the notion would apply to a transcendent being? And, even if we can somehow make that leap, why should we suppose that divine and human knowing would be relevantly similar? These questions answer themselves.

In short, objectivity has nothing to do with imaginative reconstructions of what a perfect being would know. The pursuit of objectivity, of a God's eye view, stems from what is perhaps the most human of all traits: the fact that we want and need reasons for what we believe and do. Because we abhor absurdity, we seek meaningfulness wherever we can find it. This fact of human nature is central to each of the accounts of religion we have encountered. It was a quest for meaning, human meaning, that drove the Young Hegelian project. Durkheim insisted that our collective existence—and therefore the existence of our species, inasmuch as individual human beings cannot survive alone—depends on shared meanings. In *Civilization and Its Discontents*, where the argument of *The Future of an Illusion* is continued, Freud made much of this human need, elaborating insightfully and elegantly on its several forms. Nietzsche was of one mind with the others. Characteristically, however, he gave the point an anti-Christian spin. In Christian theology, the root cause of original sin and therefore of humanity's abject condition is pride—manifest in man's attempt to take God's place by supplying meanings to God's creation. Turning this doctrine on its head, Nietzsche imputed to the superman (the *Übermensch*) the task of providing meanings—not objective meanings, for there are none, but meanings relative to his own desires and aims. In this way, he *endorsed* original sin as a condition for the possibility of the order *Übermenschen* will someday forge.

However, Nietzsche's account of what it is to legislate meanings was too egoistic to serve his purpose. Pursuing one's own good, without taking the good of others into account, will not bring meaning into the world. This has been clear, at least implicitly, for millennia. Nietzsche may have been right in attributing the first intimations of the idea, in ethical contexts, to the Jewish prophets and then to Christian thinkers. But it was not only in ancient Israel that the realization dawned that, for important subcategories of beliefs and actions, the best reasons are those that are compelling for oneself and others equally—reasons that apply to knowers and agents as such. Reasons of this kind are *justifications*, arguments of the sort that the philosophers of Greek antiquity, as much or more than the prophets of ancient Israel, sought to provide. It is because we human beings can and do justify ourselves that we are able to lead meaningful lives, notwithstanding the meaninglessness of the universe we inhabit; lives that reflect objectively defensible purposes. No imaginary deity decrees these purposes. As rational beings, driven to find compelling reasons for our beliefs and actions, we (usually unwittingly) construct them for ourselves when and insofar as we justify ourselves to ourselves and to each other.

*   *   *

Nietzsche was right to maintain that the moral point of view depends on impartial justifications. We can see why by reflecting on distinctively *moral* conceptions of justice. They revolve around what is perhaps the most primordial moral ideal: *fairness*. Whatever Nietzsche may have thought, a notion of fairness underlies even his own conception of justice.

Since Aristotle, it has been clear that the fundamental principle that appeals to justice is that like cases should be treated alike.[19] This is only a formal requirement, however; it says nothing about what counts as a like case or what equal treatment involves. To be useful in deliberative contexts, the formal principle must be supplemented by substantive principles that give it content. Examples associated with political orientations Nietzsche opposed include "to each according to need" and "to each according to productive contribution." "To each according to merit" is another substantive principle of justice, one that Nietzsche implicitly embraced and adapted to accord with his insistence on the reality of ethically relevant differences among people. This is why he thought it not only unseemly but also unjust for the mighty and the powerless to be subject to the same laws; differences in *intrinsic* merit warrant differences in treatment.

Nietzsche also seems to have believed that human differences are so great, at least between the most meritorious and everyone else, that there is no call for those at the top to justify themselves to anyone other than themselves and perhaps also to their peers, if they have any; and also that, to be true to their natures, incipient *Übermenschen* need take no interest in what lesser persons might say in their own behalf. Lions do not justify themselves to their prey. But if Nietzsche's account of intrinsic merit is wrong, then there *is* a need, in at least some instances, for *everyone* to justify themselves not just by appealing to their own interests, egoistically conceived, but to everyone's interests, including their own, impartially. It goes without saying that Nietzsche's view of intrinsic merit is wrong, if only because there are no observable, ostensibly pertinent facts that can be marshaled in its defense. But however that may be, it is plain that egoistic reflections can never rise to the level of justifications; impartial arguments are indispensable for that.

* * *

Morality is not the only idea that has a religious ancestry or that appeared initially in a theistic form; almost all major advances in our thinking, both theoretical and practical, did. That this is so is beyond dispute; the question is what to make of it beyond corroboration for Comte's (and implicitly Durkheim's) account of history's epochal phases. There are defenders of religion who invoke the theistic origins of much of what secularists believe as a mark in favor of theism. Nietzsche thought otherwise; and he was not alone.

Hegelians, some of whom were atheists, and positivists, many more of whom were, not only acknowledged the theistic origins of much of what they took to be true; the atheists among them endeavored to account for this fact. Feuerbach's case was exemplary; as we have seen, he developed what he took to be a general theory of everything by interpreting theistic ideas. That theory was a philosophical anthropology, an account of what is essentially human. Feuerbach arrived at his conception of the human essence by interpreting the Right Hegelian (Christian, Protestant, Lutheran) conception of God, while positivists got their conception of science out of the theological distortions of the past. In comparison, it seems almost trifling to "discover" moral theory by liberating the moral point of view from the theistic carapace of the Golden Rule or the prophetic utterances that preceded it.

As a "genealogist" of morality and of other ideas purportedly undone by the death of God, Nietzsche made too much of these historical connections. He mistook lines of descent for conceptual linkages. His mistake was the mirror opposite of the one made by those who acquiesce in their own bad faith by deeming theism wise—and true "in some sense"—for having given rise to ideas that secularists nowadays accept. In both cases, an historical connection is recast as a conceptual affinity that, for good or ill, can never be outgrown.

*   *   *

Nietzsche erred in making too much of morality's origins and, along with it, the origins of the democratic turn in the political culture of the modern period. But the core normative commitment implicit in his thinking, his dedication to authenticity, is unaffected by his unsuccessful case against morality and, more generally, against objectivity as an ideal. This is why we who reject Nietzschean politics categorically—who defend democracy, equality, fraternity, and other political implications of the moral point of view—can welcome Nietzsche's efforts to bring authenticity into political consciousness, notwithstanding the genealogy of *this* advance in enlightened thought.

Nietzsche deployed this standard, but he did not name it or analyze it. He only gestured towards a characterization that would describe it by referring back approvingly to a (largely mythical) pre-Christian past. He therefore drew on ethical intuitions that predate the moral point of view and that are distinct from it, but which, despite his insistence to the contrary, are compatible with it. Because it focuses on (universal) principles, moral theory differs from other strains of ethical thinking. But all strains of ethical thought, moral theory included, acknowledge the importance of virtue, and, apart from the few exceptions Nietzsche made much of, all more or less agree on what the virtues are. Ethicists throughout history have especially prized honesty. Nietzsche appropriated that consensus, generalized it, and then applied it not just to individuals' characters but, more broadly, to entire states of affairs. Whatever is true to its nature is honest in the relevant way, and therefore estimable. Whatever misrepresents itself is worthy of the condemnation that dishonesty deserves. And just as dishonesty—the pathological, not the boldly villainous, kind—elicits contempt, so does inauthenticity. Theistic convictions fail on this account. As all but the most benighted believers in the modern era understand in the deepest recesses of their minds, even as many of them deceive themselves on this account, the theism they profess is not what it seems. No matter how sincere they may be, they do not *really* believe what they claim they do. For those who would face reality squarely and with as much transparency as the human mind can attain, dishonesty of this sort warrants shame—the ultimate reproach in Nietzsche's ethical vision. The charge applies to all believers—left, right, and center—whose faith is bad faith, and therefore to all but the most involuntarily unenlightened adherents of Abrahamic faiths.

Nietzsche might not have cared to admit it, but the nihilistic project he defended assumes the distinctively *moral* injunction that underlies the Enlightenment goal of facing reality squarely, of "daring to know." On this point, Feuerbach, Durkheim, Freud, and Nietzsche were of one mind: if anything, Nietzsche was even more adamant than the others in insisting that, as a matter of *principle*, we free ourselves from our "self-imposed nonage," the better to face a world without God as it truly is. How ironic that the thinker whom some credit with undoing the Enlightenment project should be the one to give definitive expression to the normative commitment upon which it is based!

CHAPTER FIVE

THE LIBERAL TURN

Before the modern era, full-blooded faith, the genuine article, was the norm. Bad faith is the norm now. It is far from clear that full-blooded faith is even possible today, except perhaps in truly benighted quarters. Nevertheless, everywhere where Abrahamic religions remain consequential, zealotry is on the rise. Ironically, the charge of bad faith pertains more clearly to manifestations of theistic conviction that are not zealous than to those that are, and it applies not at all to those who have yet to hear the news of God's demise. Full-blooded faith or its modern approximations are worse, often much worse, in their consequences than forms of faith that are objectionable mainly on bad faith grounds. It is therefore a sign of moral progress that a normative standard that enlightened thinking has brought to the fore has become the main reproach to which much contemporary religiosity is susceptible. It shows that, in a sense broad enough to allow for significant backsliding, enlightenment is indeed taking hold.

Feuerbach, Durkheim, Freud, and Nietzsche looked forward to a time when theistic convictions would survive only in historical memory. Nietzsche focused more directly on this prospect than the others, but even he could only intimate what might arise after the nihilist project he embarked upon will have run its course. However, it was clearer to him than to the others—except perhaps Freud, who was less inclined to speculate on possible futures—that the transition from *here* to *there*, from where humanity now is (and has been for a long time) to a world beyond faith, cannot be as immediate or direct as Hegelians and positivists imagined. The goal is achievable; it may even be inevitable. But the path forward is arduous, with diversions and setbacks likely for a long time to come.

From a political point of view, full-blooded faith is almost always deleterious, and ordinary bad faith is often not far behind. But, as faith declines in intensity, it becomes less harmful; in rare circumstances, it can even be beneficial. Many factors have caused faith to wane in recent centuries, but one in particular stands out. As a rule (admitting many exceptions), the more plainly inauthentic faith is, the harder it becomes for believers to deceive themselves, the less intensely believers believe and therefore the less harmful the consequences of their beliefs become.

The liberal turn in Abrahamic religiosity is both a consequence and a cause of the transition from full-blooded faith to more anodyne varieties. It is also why bad faith sometimes serves worthwhile ends. This too is ironic. Throughout their histories, the Abrahamic religions, with their pretensions to exclusivity, have long promoted one or another form of intolerance—in religious matters especially, but in other aspects of life as well. Since liberalism is a philosophy of tolerance, of *laissez-vivre*, one would expect the Abrahamic religions to resist taking on a liberal coloration. However, in accommodating to modern conditions, some of their adherents have adopted liberal ideas in ways that mitigate the harmful political consequences of their beliefs. What should we make of this unlikely development?

*   *   *

In *The Decline and Fall of the Roman Empire*, Edmund Gibbon, speaking of the time when the Roman Empire flourished, observed that "the various modes of worship that prevailed in the Roman world were all considered by the people as equally true; by the philosopher as equally false; and by the magistrate as equally useful."[1] Thus there was a kind of "religious concord," as Gibbon put it. Monotheistic Judaism in distant Palestine was the exception; it promoted intolerance of paganism and its rituals. Even before it became an official religion of the Roman Empire, Christianity universalized the intolerance of its ancestor faith. It maintained that its God is the only God, and that outside its Church, there is no salvation. Thus what began as an exceptional phenomenon in a remote province spread throughout the Roman Empire, upsetting the concord Gibbon praised.

There is no turning back to pagan ways, nor should there be. But neither should we deny the fact that, in many respects, the transition from polytheism to monotheism was a step backwards. Because the winners write the history, it is almost universally assumed that civilization advanced when monotheism replaced polytheism. But, as Gibbon pointed out, Greco-Roman polytheism was less pernicious than the Abrahamic religions that succeeded it in at least one key respect: its acceptance of diversity. Nevertheless, the founders of the Abrahamic faiths and their successors were right in holding that polytheistic beliefs are not worthy of serious consideration. Unfortunately, it took just a few centuries shy of two millennia for a comparable judgment to be leveled against their own beliefs. It is even more unfortunate that this incontrovertible conclusion remains a minority view nearly everywhere to this day.

In Greco-Roman antiquity, tolerance proceeded from a general recognition of the fact that beliefs are local—or, more precisely, as Durkheim would later explain, tied to particular social groups. In the modern period, under the aegis of an increasingly globalizing capitalist system, local cultures became more alike as people became citizens of nation-states that incorporated diverse social groupings. It was in these circumstances that liberalism emerged. Liberalism instilled a more robust and humane tolerance than had existed before—not because it revived respect for local customs, but because it recognized that modern states work best when religious convictions, along with other potentially divisive commitments, are treated as matters of private conscience with no direct political bearing. Each of the Abrahamic religions were, in varying degrees, able to transform themselves to accommodate this recognition. Thus liberalism's rise gave rise to liberal religion, ostensibly a new form of religiosity. But liberal religion is not so much a new form of faith as a depoliticized version of the old form; one that provides a (painfully slow) vehicle of exit for a civilization that has outgrown theism but that, for trenchant human reasons, finds itself unable unequivocally to shake off its yoke.

Liberalism insinuated itself into the Abrahamic religions—
first, into Protestant Christianity, later into Judaism, later still
into strains of Catholic and Orthodox Christianity. Islam followed suit in the early decades of the twentieth century. Ironically, Western, especially American, imperialism blocked this
development decades later, and even turned it back. By encouraging the politicization of Islam as a counterforce to secular
movements that threatened American and Western domination
of historically Muslim lands, it derailed Islam's push towards
liberalization. Liberal Islam therefore lags behind liberal Christianity and liberal Judaism. Where liberal religion is a viable
alternative to secularism, one can be both tolerant and religious.
In the Islamic world, this unlikely configuration has become
more difficult to achieve. There are some who bemoan this situation and others who advocate rectifying it. However, the
absence of a robust liberal alternative to secularism may ultimately be an advantage in the struggle to see through and
beyond theistic ideas. In the long run, liberal religion is a transitional phase on the way to irreligion. This phase can linger for
a very long time. Surely, it is better to leap over it entirely than
to succumb to its temptations. Since the eighteenth century, if
not before, many Christians and Jews have done precisely that.
Many Muslims have, too. It may seem unlikely in today's world
but it is nevertheless fair to conjecture that, in a not too distant
future, the absence of a robust liberal pole of attraction may
actually make it easier for persons born in Muslim cultures than
for others to "take consciousness" of what ought to follow from
the fact of God's demise.

The liberal turn has never come easily. Abrahamic faiths

resist liberalization, though, with the partial exception of Islam, they have been able to reinvent themselves to incorporate liberal tenets into their fold. They did not do so for theologically principled reasons, at least at first. Reasons have been provided in retrospect, of course, but what ultimately explains liberal religion is a felt, though unacknowledged, need on the part of generally enlightened people, for whom irreligion is not yet a viable option, to back away from positions that assume God still lives. This is why when religions assume a liberal form, it is a sign of the waning of faith.

*   *   *

Liberalism emerged in Western Europe in the aftermath of the Protestant Reformation and the wars of religion to which it gave rise. Spurred by the teachings of church reformers, entrepreneurial political elites and dissident clerics backed by fervent followers forged ecclesiastical structures free from the institutional and theological control of Rome. The Roman Catholic Church was at least as determined as the reformers to hold power, and the Catholic populations of contested territories were no less fervent. The Roman Church had, from its inception, proclaimed itself indispensable for salvation, savagely repressing those it declared heretical or schismatic, while periodically unleashing violence against pagans and Jews and, later, Muslims. By maintaining that the papacy had forfeited its legitimacy, the Protestant Churches that broke away from Rome made similar claims for themselves and evinced similar intolerance. Thus, on matters of the utmost concern to the parties involved, the positions of the contending groups, Catholics and Protestant, were irreconcilable. There was nothing for them to do, therefore, but take up arms against each other: to compel their enemies to come over to their own side or, if that proved impossible, to eliminate them by force. The consequences were devastating.

In time, however, the competing sides, having fought to exhaustion, became increasingly inclined to accept each other's practices and beliefs, albeit grudgingly. Nearly everywhere, a *modus vivendi* developed—at first between political entities ruled by leaders committed to different confessions and then, in territories with mixed populations, within political communities as well. Thus, throughout Western Christendom, religious tolerance, missing since Greco-Roman antiquity, reemerged. In time, European thinkers and some European populations, along with their counterparts in North America, came to view tolerance as a political virtue. The idea that its range of application should extend not just to religious conflicts but also to all matters of political consequence followed. What began as a reluctant and narrowly focused willingness to forbear from imposing religious beliefs on others evolved into a positive value that people enthusiastically endorsed. Correspondingly, in philosophical circles, the idea emerged that a good society is a tolerant society; and therefore that there are reasons for tolerance that go beyond the need to keep peace between intolerant religious sects.

This idea, that tolerance is a political virtue, defines liberalism. From the beginning, this conviction was joined with efforts to develop the modern state form of political organization. In feudal societies, political authority was decentralized—in practice, if not always in theory. In some times and places, kings or emperors reigned, at least officially. However, for the most part, feudal lords exercised actual political and economic power. In contrast, the modern state concentrates all political authority—all rights to compel compliance through the use or threat of force—into a single institutional nexus. This sovereign power exercises what Max Weber famously called "a monopoly of the means of (legitimate) violence."[2]

It was therefore only natural that justifying theories of the state at first recognized no restrictions on the sovereign's power, holding that sovereignty is, by its nature, unlimited or absolute. Thomas Hobbes's account in *The Leviathan* provided the clearest and certainly the most influential example. Tellingly, Hobbes argued that absolute power is necessary for suppressing threats to civil order including those posed by religious diversity. In his view, the sovereign can rightfully make definitive rulings in doctrinal disputes and may enforce his decisions by whatever means he deems suitable.[3] Proponents of religious toleration, though drawn to the Hobbesian notion of sovereignty, nevertheless insisted that state interventions in religious matters are incompatible both with good governance and support for individuals' rights, and must therefore be proscribed. They therefore endorsed restrictions on the sovereign's power. In doing so, they assumed the burden of developing justifying theories of the state that did not also justify absolute authority on the sovereign power's part. By the later decades of the seventeenth century, a number of thinkers had risen to the occasion; among the most

influential was John Locke. He and other early liberals concocted theories of limited sovereignty. Inasmuch as they
assumed that persons are free to do whatever the sovereign
does not proscribe, their theories of limited sovereignty were
also, in effect, theories of individual liberty.

Early liberals were able to draw on the theoretical
resources absolutist philosophers bequeathed them because
the most trenchant defenders of absolutism, like Hobbes,
already acknowledged a presumption against coercive interference with individuals' lives and behaviors. Hobbes
defended "negative liberty," the absence of coercive restraint.
Implicitly, therefore, he regarded restrictions on liberty as
necessary evils, requiring justification. That was a task Hobbes
and liberals after him assumed, showing how the presumption
against coercive interference can be, and typically is, overridden. The argument, in brief, is just that without any coercion at all, there could be no state; a condition even worse
than one in which negative liberty is to some extent restricted.
On this point, Hobbes and the liberals agreed.

They all wanted an optimal level of negative liberty—as
much as there can be without succumbing to a devastating war
of all against all. Hobbes thought that the only way to avoid
that worst of all possible outcomes was to invest unrestricted
power in a sovereign. He acknowledged a presumption against
coercive interference but insisted that it could be overridden
at the sovereign's pleasure. On this point, proponents of
absolute authority and liberal proponents of limited sovereignty parted ways. Liberals hold that there are things even
sovereigns cannot rightfully do. Their thought, variously

defended, is that there is a private sphere of individuals' lives and behaviors into which the state may not rightfully intrude. There was, and still is, controversy over what falls into the private sphere. By all accounts, freedom of expression does, along with freedom of the press and freedom of assembly—though precisely what these freedoms involve has always been controversial. Economic activities associated with the untrammeled accumulation of private property are more controversial still, though the first liberals, including Locke, were as intent on rendering these activities immune from state interference as they were devoted to religious toleration. To this day, the status of economic freedoms divides the liberal camp. But there has never been any doubt that religious beliefs and practices should be immune from state interference or favor. Born in reaction to the consequences of religious strife, liberalism has always been true to its origins.

To be sure, some early liberals courted inconsistency by supporting the establishment of state churches. Their dedication to state-building effectively trumped their liberal scruples. That there should be an established church was the dominant view in Great Britain and in the northern European countries, though not in the United States. Even so, the idea that *all* religious expression should be treated fairly, if not quite equally, was inherent in the liberal creed. State power must never be used to enforce religious orthodoxy even when there are established churches, and it must never be used to suppress religious expressions of any kind. In the face of long-standing traditions of intolerance, grounded in fundamental theological convictions, it required a protracted struggle for this core tenet of liberal theory to win the day. It required struggle, too, to extend liberal protections to deists and Jews and, in time, also to atheists and agnostics. Inexorably, though, religious convictions of all kinds found their way into the private sphere. As this process unfolded, the changes in thinking it encouraged were far-reaching enough to bring other liberal protections along and to reinforce liberal attitudes generally.

Defenses of limited sovereignty only concern individuals' relations to the state. In due course, the view emerged that the private sphere ought to be expanded to include *societal* interferences as well. Tolerance therefore became a social, not just a political, virtue and ultimately a personal one as well. Thus, from the late eighteenth century on, the consensus view among liberals came to be that good societies are comprised of people disposed in their interactions with others scrupulously to respect the boundaries of an expansive and robust private sphere, and that the political and social institutions that regulate their lives should treat all religious expressions fairly.

*   *   *

It was inevitable, in these circumstances, that liberalism should make inroads into the Abrahamic religions. When this happened, it was, at first, often for opportunistic reasons. Those who had the most to gain from fair treatment by political authorities took it upon themselves to defend tolerance within their own theological traditions. Theologically driven justifications for tolerance were therefore developed first within subaltern denominations in England, the Lowlands, and German-speaking parts of western and central Europe. Following their lead, it became clear, in due course, that all but the most "catholic" of Protestant sects could liberalize their theologies. For Protestants, the Bible is the supreme authority on matters of religious (and sometimes extra-religious) conviction, and no church is equipped to interpret it infallibly. Protestant sects disagreed on how much credence to place in the interpretations of their respective authorities. But they all accorded preeminence to individual conscience, some going so far as to maintain that it is the ultimate authority on Biblical truth. It was then natural to go on to hold that interferences with the operations of private conscience are detrimental to sound religion. By this reasoning, tolerance became a theologically grounded requirement and therefore also a religious virtue—in addition to a political, social, and personal one.

Thanks to its precarious position within the Roman Empire in the first several centuries of its existence, and then thanks to the deteriorating conditions of European political institutions as the Roman Empire fell apart, Christianity had always acknowledged a distinction between temporal and ecclesiastical authority. The distinction was reinforced throughout the Middle Ages and into the early modern period. This theological, legal, and customary division made it easier for tolerance to develop within Christian societies than in social environments shaped by the other Abrahamic faiths. Neither Judaism nor Islam had ever separated religion from politics in quite so principled a way. In the Jewish case, the difference was unimportant because Jewish communities only existed in territories Jews did not rule. The difference was more important in the Muslim world because Islam was the official religion of regimes holding sway over vast territories in Asia, Africa, Oceana, and Europe. Christian exceptionalism is a large part of the reason why, in western, northern, and central Europe, those who were disposed to turn religion into a matter of private conscience found conditions propitious. By distinguishing church and state and marking off their respective realms, Christianity enabled the emergence of the idea that states should be neutral in contests between competing churches—and the further claim that tolerance is a positive good, not a necessary evil that can be set aside whenever it is feasible to do so. After that idea became established, it was not too great a leap to the conclusion that religious diversity is good not just for ethical, political, and social reasons, but for religious reasons as well. But how can that thought coexist with the idea, inherent in Abrahamic religiosity, that only one's own faith is true?

Liberal Protestant theologians were the first to square the circle or, rather, to evade the realization that the circle cannot be squared. For this, they have their place in history to thank. Waning fervor, the condition that made a *modus vivendi* between competing sects possible, made liberal religion possible, too. Full-blooded believers are and always will be intolerant because the existence of rival views challenges the legitimacy of their own. But as salvation ceases to be a matter of genuine concern, as theological commitments become more formal than real, intolerance subsides. Liberals who identify with one or another Abrahamic tradition and who understandably want the beliefs they profess to cohere, will then welcome theological defenses of tolerance, no matter how strained their reasoning may be; and dedicated theologians will exercise all their ingenuity concocting them.

This is not to impugn the sincerity of those who took the liberal turn. The first liberal theologians were not atheists taking cover within Protestant churches. As (partial) heirs of the Enlightenment tradition, some of them may have been what David Hume called "atheists without knowing it." But even if that is what they were, the point is that they didn't know it. This is why liberal Protestantism, on their construal of it, was not cast as a dodge for those not yet ready to face reality squarely. For all intents and purposes, it was what it purported to be: a system of thought suitable to modern conditions and continuous with historical Christianity.

In this guise, it has survived for a long time and shows no sign of succumbing any time soon. But one can only doubt the permanency of a theological tendency that struggles to reconcile tolerance and exclusivity—the one, a creature of the modern, secular age; the other, a hallmark of religions that have wrought havoc throughout their entire existence for the sake of the One True God. Doubts about the indefinite durability of the liberal turn are compounded further by the fact that liberal religion is both a consequence and a cause of waning faith. Liberal faith is weak. One must therefore wonder whether it can adequately address the needs that give faith its (meretricious) appeal; whether it is up to the task of serving as an opium of the people.

In turning Christianity away from its intolerant core and moving it in a more liberal direction, Hegel's philosophy of religion played a role. Hegel maintained that religion and philosophy are alternative routes to the same end—the one working through myths and symbols, the other through theses and arguments. This contention licensed Right Hegelianism; its proponents, theologians all, recast Hegelian positions in theological terms. The idea that there are two roads to the same end, one of them theological, the other not, courts inauthenticity. But Hegel and his followers arguably avoided this charge because they assumed, more or less explicitly, that, in the backward and still barely literate Germany of their time, only a handful of people would be able to achieve self-consciousness through philosophy alone. For them, Christianity functioned like the Golden Lie in Plato's *Republic*, a myth that serves reason's purpose when reason cannot be fully in control. However, conditions have changed—not just in Germany, but everywhere. Backwardness is no longer an excuse. The point is perfectly general. Where enlightened ideas are accessible not just to a few philosophically precocious elites but to everyone in the ambient intellectual culture, theistic faith is bad faith; and the liberal turn, which gives bad faith its distinctively modern form, is a condition for its possibility.

*   *   *

Liberal Protestantism influenced liberal (Reform) Judaism substantially, though the way forward for Jews was not quite

175

the same as for Christians. Unlike Christianity, Judaism had never made doctrinal orthodoxy central to its understanding of piety; piety always had more to do with the observance of religious laws. Thus Judaism is comparatively undemanding theologically. It was therefore easier for liberal Jews than for liberal Christians to maintain theological continuity with co-religionists, and it was possible too, at this level, for liberal Jews to make common cause with liberal Protestants. But Reform Judaism's myths and symbols were different from those of the reformed churches; and, on this point, there could be no compromise. Liberal Protestants drew on Christian traditions. A people that Christendom had persecuted from its earliest days and whom Christians continued to persecute could hardly find Christian motifs congenial. This was one reason why there were limits to how much like liberal Protestantism Reform Judaism could become; another, of greater moment in philosophical circles in Germany at the time, was that Jewish myths and symbols were understood to have been deployed for a different purpose than Christianity's—or, rather, Christianity's as conceived within the tradition of classical German philosophy. Hegel and his followers, and some of his predecessors too, thought that Christianity gave mythic expression to the ideas philosophy advanced. However plausible (or not) this understanding may be, it made little sense, by their lights and therefore also to the founders of the Reform movement, to say the same of Judaism. The reason is not just that Christianity represents a "higher" form of religious experience or that its myths and symbols somehow parallel the theses and arguments with which Hegel purportedly brought philosophy itself to its end. The main reason is that, in fact (as well as in the thinking of German theologians) Jewish myths and symbols have never had much to do with anything that could plausibly be identified with philosophical positions, Hegelian or otherwise. They served instead to rationalize a legal system comprised of commandments and prohibitions that regulate both the sacred realm and ordinary life of the Jewish people. This is what had defined Jewish piety for millennia, and it is what had to be abandoned or, at least, severely curtailed for liberal Judaism to come into being.

A robustly liberal political culture demands that religion be a matter of private conscience only; that it have no distinct political or social standing. Practices governed by rules that apply to some citizens and not others are therefore problematic. This is the main reason why Reform Judaism sought to abandon Jewish law. Reform Jews observed Jewish holidays and recited some of the traditional prayers, sometimes in Hebrew, the traditional liturgical language. But they no longer observed the dietary laws or abstained from activity on the Sabbath; indeed they did as little as possible, outside their temples (the new name for synagogues) to set themselves apart from their fellow citizens. Christianity had abandoned the law on the grounds that, with Christ's death and resurrection, the old order had been superseded. Obviously, Reform Judaism could have none of that. It abandoned the law because the observances it prescribed were incompatible with participation in modern social and political life, and because a philosophical commitment to liberalism justified assimilation in all matters not pertaining to private beliefs. Thus it was for liberal reasons that Reform Judaism in its "classical" phase actively promoted the pale semblance of Jewish tradition that it has continued to maintain ever since.

In time, circumstances triumphed over philosophical conviction. Particularly in the United States, the theory behind Reform Judaism became diluted; then what remained was just the practice (or lack of it) that the theory recommended. This led some of the intellectual descendants of the liberals who had founded the Reform movement to abandon the faith altogether—in some cases, going so far as to join Protestant sects like the Unitarians or the Friends. Others developed secular versions of what Reform Judaism had endeavored to become; the Ethical Culture movement is an example. Meanwhile, as Reform Judaism attracted new members, its moorings in liberal theory became increasingly attenuated. It is relevant that the demographics of the Reform movement changed, especially after World War II, when it turned into an almost exclusively North American phenomenon. Before World War II, Reform Judaism's North American contingent had been comprised mainly of assimilated Jews of German origin who had arrived in the United States and Canada several generations before the waves of late nineteenth- and early twentieth-century migrations from central and eastern Europe. Anti-Semitism kept even the most successful Jews from integrating fully into the highest echelons of Protestant society. But nothing prevented them from developing parallel institutions and interacting with Protestant elites on a separate but more or less equal basis. In time, as class divisions between German and central and eastern European Jews faded, and as the Jews of central and eastern Europe who had emigrated to the New World assimilated, they joined the Reform movement in large numbers. With these new recruits driving the agenda, Reform congregations began to reintegrate elements of traditional Jewish practice.

But no one attracted to Reform Judaism wanted to revive the archaic legalisms of pre-emancipated Jewish life. This is why, as traditional Left and liberal values have gone into eclipse or fallen under the sway of identity politics, a remarkable transformation has occurred within Reform ranks. Even as assimilation proceeds at full-throttle, the assimilationist ideal was abandoned. What made this possible was identification with Zionism and, later, the Israeli state. There is much that is odious in this development and very little that is of spiritual moment. But, for many diaspora Jews, Zionism offered a way to retain a Jewish identity without relinquishing the benefits of modernity or taking on the burdens of observance. Ironically, the Zionist turn coincided with a subsidence of institutional and attitudinal anti-Semitism. As American Jews integrated thoroughly into American life, neither long-standing Christian hostility nor its racial offshoots any longer reinforced a sense of Jewish identity. Apart from the tribalistic mentality inherent in a religion that sees its adherents as God's chosen people, there was nothing except Zionism that could serve this purpose. Originally, Reform Judaism took little interest in Jewish identity, in part because it was genuinely liberal and therefore committed to a universalistic and cosmopolitan worldview, but also because, at the time of its inception, Jewish distinctiveness was not in doubt. The

problem was not to sustain Jewish identity, much less to man-
ufacture it, but to forge bonds of common citizenship between
Christians and Jews. This is why, decades ago, most Reform
Jews opposed the Zionist project, though a few did grudgingly
accept the idea because they thought that there ought to be a
refuge in Palestine (by then, the settled location) for Jews
whose prospects for survival in Europe were bleak. It could
hardly have been otherwise; the very idea of a confessional or
ethnic state is inimical to liberal convictions, a fact that
somehow passes unnoticed in most liberal circles today. However, in the aftermath of the Nazi Judeocide and after a Jewish
state in Palestine had become a *fait accompli*, all Jewish ten-
dencies, apart from a few Orthodox sects, succumbed to the
Zionist temptation. The Reform movement had a principled
reason to distance itself from this eventuality. But it was not
immune.

*   *   *

The Roman Catholic hierarchy found ways to adapt to liberalism as circumstances required. Having opposed aspects of
modernity until well into the twentieth century, the Second
Vatican Council culminated a gradual transformation through
which the Church, ever resilient, succeeded in accommodating
itself to the increasingly secular and liberal political cultures of
Western Europe and North America. Unintentionally, it also
encouraged more radical strains of Catholic theory and practice. During the first half of the twentieth century, first in
France, later in the United States where a Catholic workers'

movement developed, and, later still, throughout Europe and Latin America, the Catholic Church became a home for faith-based left-wing political movements. In the 1960s and '70s, there were American priests, nuns, and members of religious orders actively involved in opposition to the Vietnam War and other progressive causes. By the 1980s, Catholics were conspicuous in solidarity movements for popular struggles in Africa and Central and South America, making common cause with the "liberation theologians" and dissident clergies of the global South. These were phenomena of the base; the Church hierarchy remained opposed. Moreover, the political formations supported by these intraecclesiastical insurgencies, though friendly to liberal concerns, were animated by Left values that transcended the horizons of traditional liberalism. They were, however, cut from the same cloth.

As remarked, in the Muslim world, full-fledged secularism, not liberal religion, was the main alternative to traditional faith. Lacking political traditions conducive to liberal practice, this was probably inevitable. Attempts to liberalize Islam foundered too on the fact that liberalism is linked, historically and conceptually, to the political cultures of the Muslim world's oppressors. With the emergence of political Islam in recent decades, there have been calls aplenty, especially from non-Muslims, for the liberalization of the faith. But, for the reasons that impeded the rise of liberal Islam in the past, this will likely not come to pass. The consequences could be dire. On the other hand, if imperialist predations can be made to diminish, causing political Islam's appeal to fade, the Muslim world could find itself in a uniquely favorable situation. More easily than in cultures shaped by Judaism or Christianity, Muslim peoples should be able to leap over the long transitional phase of liberal religion, reacting more authentically than liberal believers do to the fact that God is dead.

*   *   *

As long as outright irreligious alternatives continue to be discouraged by prevailing norms, liberal religion will probably survive, especially where liberalism is an indigenous ideology. But because liberal religions sequester faith into an apolitical private sphere, encouraging personal and group identifications that fall outside the purview of private conscience, their efficacy as opiates of the people is limited. They therefore open up space for more full-blooded expressions of religiosity. Being suitable only for those of little faith, liberal religion invites the reemergence of more atavistic forms of religiosity in times and places where the need for a more effective opiate arises. Feuerbach recognized this shortcoming when liberal religion was still in its infancy. This is one reason why he concluded that, no matter how important freedom of religion is for modern states, and no matter how appealing liberal religion may be for some people, what is needed ultimately is freedom from religion. Liberal religion is a palliative for persons unable fully to come to terms with a world reshaping itself in the aftermath of God's death; it provides them with a venue for exercising bad faith. This is objectionable in its own right, but it is also untenable in the long run. The alternatives, Feuerbach insisted, are enslavement to a narcotizing religiosity or, as true freedom implies, facing reality as it is. Liberal religion is not an alternative; there is no third way. Nothing has changed in this regard since Feuerbach's time: the alternatives remain the ones he plotted out.

It can seem otherwise. But this impression is a result of a confluence of fortuitous historical accidents. In post-Reformation Europe, circumstances conspired to diminish the baleful effects of Abrahamic religiosity. That sensibility was exported to Protestant North America and then throughout the world. It was taken up by Jews eager for political and social emancipation. It has remained in force wherever memories of Europe's sectarian conflicts endure. Since the countries where these memories are most intense came to dominate the rest of the world, liberalism became a pole of attraction everywhere. Thus it migrated into all the Abrahamic faiths—though only recently into strains of Christianity that were in the forefront of resistance to modernity, and only barely into the Islamic fold.

But the world is changing in ways that force attention upon the ultimately transitory nature of the liberal turn; historical memories fade, the victims of colonial and postcolonial oppression assert themselves, and people migrate into liberalism's heartlands from regions with more theocratic traditions, bringing more noxious forms of religiosity with them. Then the feasibility of liberal religion becomes increasingly problematic, hopes for a third way founder, and the real alternatives stand starkly revealed. In the first decades of the twenty-first century, as in the world the Young Hegelians inhabited, the choice is becoming ever more clear: if reason does not prevail, intolerance and strife will.

The fact that Western Europe, the birthplace of liberal religion, is now largely secular gives reason for hope that the liberal turn need not be a dead end; that it can be a stage on the way to a truly post-theistic world. But as imperialist depredations generate ever more dangerous conditions in parts of the world prone to theocratic eruptions, the prospects for the immediate future are far from hopeful. The fact that it enables so many people to be in bad faith is reason enough to militate against liberal religion, but there is a more pressing political reason as well. Liberal religion itself may be relatively harmless, but it cannot be counted on to provide a bulwark against intolerance and other consequences of later-day approximations of full-blooded faith. Decades ago, when the way forward seemed inexorable, no one would have imagined that the world could fall back into a new Dark Age. But, as circumstances become increasingly desperate, this is happening—not just in historically Muslim precincts but everywhere. Longstanding secular regimes are not immune. Even the United States, a nation brought into being by enlightened thinkers but now lagging behind most of Europe on the path to secularization, is vulnerable.

There is, however, another possibility, available as much or more to peoples whom liberal religion has barely touched as to those who have long been in its comparatively benign grip. There is the prospect, envisioned by Feuerbach, Durkheim, Freud, and Nietzsche, among a host of others, that, by casting off its Abrahamic remnants, humankind will profoundly and irreversibly emancipate itself from its "self-imposed nonage." It is urgent that this comes to pass.

CHAPTER SIX

A PRECARIOUS LEFT

Liberalism severed the connection between membership in a faith community and political status; in this respect, it depoliticized religion. But it permits the faithful to advance political objectives consistent with convictions it relegates to the private sphere. The liberal turn therefore brought religion back in—making it possible for theistic beliefs to lead individuals to identify with any of a variety of political currents, including some to the left of liberalism itself. Thus there have been currents within the Abrahamic fold that identify with the political Left. The causes for their rise are, for the most part, specific to particular times and places. I will not dwell on those causes, nor will I focus on the differences between various expressions of Left religiosity. I will consider them all together under one broad designation. Liberal versions of Abrahamic religions share common philosophical commitments and are part of the same historical tendency. This is arguably less true of the constituent elements of the religious Left. Nevertheless, their resemblances are salient enough to group them together.

The religious Left has done much that is estimable. Even so, it is obvious, I think, that, from a political point of view, the good that faith inspires hardly begins to counter the harm it has done and continues to do. I will not attempt to defend that contention; that would be a fool's errand. Even were it feasible to compare harms and benefits according to some plausible metric, it would never be possible to identify all the relevant benefits and harms, and it would always be controversial precisely what to take into account.

It bears repeating that, in the modern era, the more benign forms of faith, including those that do more good than harm, exhibit bad faith. Those who militate for Left causes on religious grounds run afoul of this charge as much as other believers do. All the faithful, except truly benighted ones, stand indicted. It bears repeating too that, though insincerity is rampant, sincerity is not the issue. Adherence to one or another religion is more reflexive than heartfelt for many self-identified believers; the world is therefore full of persons whose faith is both inauthentic and insincere. In this respect, the religious Left stands apart; its militants are almost always sincere. But sincerity no more absolves those who are on "the side of the angels" than it does believers on the other side, whether they be deluded ideologues or only victims of social or political circumstances so dire that the intensity of their beliefs rises to full-blooded levels.

The religious Left is a creature of the liberal turn. But unlike liberal religion generally, it warrants attention not so much because of its consequences for religious thought or its effects on real history, but because its very existence focuses attention on the inherent political bearing of the Abrahamic faiths. Reflecting on that issue brings another problem with the religious Left to light: its especially precarious nature.

*　　*　　*

I suggested in the last chapter that liberal religion is a transitional phenomenon, albeit one that has existed for several centuries and that will likely survive for a long time to come. Left religiosity is therefore a transitional phenomenon too; in part because, like liberal religion generally, its narcotizing potentialities are too feeble to endure indefinitely. But other strains of liberal religiosity are at least philosophically coherent; left religiosity, in contrast, joins together a contradictory configuration of values and positions. Religious Lefts are therefore unlikely to survive continuously for extended periods of time, though new manifestations may arise occasionally for as long as "faith perspectives" remain with us. In support of this conjecture, it will be instructive to compare the core ideas of the political Left with ostensibly similar notions of Abrahamic provenance.

From the time of the French Revolution, when the more radical delegates to the National Assembly seated themselves to the left of the presiding officer, *Left* has designated a relatively stable, though evolving and multifaceted, political orientation dedicated, in the words of the French revolutionary slogan, to "liberty, equality, and fraternity." These aspirations were not exactly new. But the Left's purchase on them was. A political Left is a modern phenomenon. It would have been impossible without the state form of political organization, according to which political authority is vested in a single institutional nexus; without at least a semblance of popular control over state institutions; and without the idea that morality's scope extends to the basic institutions that govern individuals' lives. These conditions shaped Left conceptions of liberty, equality, and fraternity, severing some of the linkages with premodern understandings.

The idea that morality implies equal treatment on the part of basic societal institutions was pivotal. As remarked, it was within nascent Christianity that the moral point of view first received a definitive, though philosophically primitive, formulation. It was proclaimed in the Golden Rule, attributed to Jesus himself. That rule counsels us to do unto others as we would have others do unto us. The intended contrast is with egoism—doing unto others whatever is best for one's self. Needless to say, in many, perhaps most, deliberative contexts, the particularity of the agent deliberating matters decisively; egoism is therefore often an appropriate deliberative stance. But not always, according to moral theorists, the intellectual descendants, as it were, of the first proponents of the Golden Rule. For them, there are circumstances in which the rightness or wrongness of actions and the goodness or badness of states of affairs can only be ascertained impartially—as the Golden Rule implies.

Ethical prohibitions and prescriptions enunciated on the authority of a (or "the") God—in, say, the Ten Commandments or in the ethical codes of other archaic peoples—are therefore alternatives to moral theory. Nevertheless, it is widely believed that these prohibitions and prescriptions comprise the content of morality. A comparatively sophisticated version of this idea is that the commandments of the gods or God are, at least in some instances, consistent with what morality requires, and that putting these requirements in commandment form makes them more accessible to believers than they would otherwise be. On this understanding and with sufficient ingenuity, one can read morality back into the ethical doctrines of almost any religion. But it would be disingenuous, at best, to claim that it was there from the start.

However, it is plausible to maintain that, whatever other ethical codes may imply, the one we associate with ancient Israel contained the seeds of a notion of human equality that the Left, some two millennia later, would make its own. It is remarkable that it took so long. After all, it is not so great a leap from the idea that everyone should count equally in ethical deliberations to the idea that human societies should be regulated according to principles that are defensible from an impartial or agent-neutral standpoint. In promoting an idea of universal human equality, the Abrahamic religions sowed the seed for moving ethical thinking forward, even as they impeded forward movement for a very long time. The ethical advance registered within the Abrahamic ambit could remain politically inert because being equal with respect to what matters fundamentally—whether it be equality in the mind of God or equality from the moral point of view, equality of pure agency—does not strictly imply a claim to equal treatment by social or political institutions. The practice of the medieval church illustrates the difference. The idea that lord and serf are of equal concern to God because they possess souls of equal worth was accepted doctrine. Yet no one imagined that this conviction implied social or political equality. Even within the church, members of different classes were treated differently—except in the exercise of certain religious obligations and in the administration of the sacraments.

Nevertheless, metaphysical conceptions matter, which is one reason why the Left emerged in historically Christian civilizations. But for it to do so, a break with Christianity was indispensable. Evidently, a similar rupture is necessary in political cultures under Islam's sway—where being on the Left has always gone hand in hand with irreligion and secularism. Much the same holds for Jews. Despite the availability of a liberal (Reform) movement within the Jewish fold, Left-leaning Jews have long been second to none in championing irreligion. In short, though it is possible to find anticipations of Left values and ideas in the Jewish, Christian, and Islamic traditions, the Left developed by breaking away from these systems of practice and belief. Those who believe that Left convictions are conceptually of a piece with Abrahamic ideas are in the thrall of an illusion in Freud's sense; their belief is an expression of a wish.

Even so, there is a segment of the Left that identifies with the core convictions Judaism, Christianity, and Islam share; and there are many on the Left who embrace the doctrinal commitments of one or another Abrahamic faith. As the traditional Left has fallen into decline and as "progressives" have become intent on winning over and perhaps even joining the ranks of the faithful, the problematic nature of Left religiosity often passes unnoticed. But it is not difficult to see that there is an opposition; or rather, since it has been clear to nearly everyone, Left and Right, for generations, to reestablish its salience.

Wherever there are similarities and differences in ideas, practices, and traditions, it is possible to concoct narratives that emphasize either continuities or discontinuities. Political considerations often play an important, sometimes a decisive, role. This case is no different. Those who want to find a place for theism within the broad Left tent emphasize affinities between the modern Left and the faith traditions with which people on the religious Left identify. Those who think that efforts to secure cohabitation are wrong-headed emphasize the differences. But, in this instance, contending narratives are not on an equal footing. The Left's purchase on its defining values—liberty, equality, and fraternity—is different enough from Abrahamic perspectives that the case for continuity is at a plain disadvantage. Needless to say, distinct and even incompatible conceptions of liberty, equality and fraternity abound even in the modern period.[1] But widely shared understandings are all we need take into account to see how theism promotes ways of thinking that are at odds with the Left's political project.

*   *   *

For a purchase on Abrahmic conceptions of liberty, it will be well to detour through the so-called argument from evil, the obverse of one of the pillars of rational theology, the argument from design. That argument purports to establish the rationality of belief in God by maintaining that the evidence of nature supports the hypothesis that God exists. The argument from evil supports the opposite hypothesis and also

191

appeals to evidence. As we have seen, the argument from design is a nonstarter. Nevertheless, it has a certain appeal insofar as it depends on the sense of awe people sometimes experience when they contemplate the complexity of nature or its component parts. However, to acquire this evidence, a certain concentration of attention is indispensable. Ordinary life stifles wonderment; it forces us to focus just on getting on. To find evidence in nature that moves persons to assent to the claim that God exists, it is therefore necessary that they enter into a receptive frame of mind. This is not the case with the argument from evil. The evidence on which it depends is too overwhelming and too ineluctable to pass unnoticed.

Reduced to its core, the argument is easily described. Deists (and therefore also theists) believe that there is an omnipotent, omniscient, and perfectly good God. But this belief is in tension with the fact that bad things happen; that there is evil. Thanks to our propensity to acquiesce, a habit of mind the Abrahamic religions encourage, standard formulations of the argument focus on extraordinary occurrences. But, as I suggested in the introduction, the deistic (and theistic) hypothesis conflicts just as much with the ordinary annoyances and infelicities of daily life. It is hard to see how anyone can get through even a few hours of life on earth without becoming aware of countless reasons for doubting that the God deists (and theists) imagine is real.

This is one reason why it is misleading to call this line of reasoning an argument from evil. Another is that "evil," the term used to designate the evidence on which the argument depends, is itself a creature of religious thought. The Abrahamic religions share the idea with their polytheistic and pretheistic ancestors; and versions of it occur in many contemporary religious traditions, not just the Abrahamic ones. But there is no need to rely on any particular theological account of what is wrong with the world to appreciate the argument's force; and if, out of respect for tradition, the word "evil" is used for this purpose, colloquial understandings are more than sufficient. In ordinary speech, and in ostensibly more scrupulous contexts as well, "evil" just means "bad" or, more usually, "very bad." This is all that the term will mean here.[2]

In short, the argument holds that the following claims are inconsistent: a) that God is omnipotent; b) that God is omniscient; c) that God is perfectly good; and d) that evil exists. Denying any one of them would, of course, undo the argument. If there were no evil, there would be no need to reconcile (a), (b), and (c) with (d). Neither would there be a problem for deists (or theists) if (a) were false; they could say that there are evils God is simply unable to quash. Similarly, if (b) were false, evils might transpire because God does not know about them; and were (c) false, the existence of evil would not be incompatible with God's nature. But denying one or another of these contentions is not a strategy that a deist (or theist) defending against the argument can deploy. It would beg the question to deny (d); and to abandon (a), (b), or (c) would be tantamount to abandoning the Abrahamic conception of God, inasmuch as (a), (b), and (c) are its main tenets. Believers must therefore find a way to reconcile God's existence with the existence of evil or else concede that their faith is irrational. The strategy those who want to avoid that charge typically adopt is to blame man. Christianity is more extreme than Judaism or Islam in doing so; though, on this point, they are all basically in accord.[3] They all agree that "free will," or rather its abuse, is the root of all evil.

When incontrovertible evidence conflicts with theologically grounded expectations, the faithful can always say that God's will is inscrutable, and leave it at that. Thus they have an answer for everything. But it is hardly a satisfactory answer, at least not for anyone who wants to make sense of the greater or lesser evils everyone everywhere confronts. For those seeking understanding, appeals to divine inscrutability ring hollow. This is why it is tempting for believers to say that we have brought our misfortunes upon ourselves. However, that answer too can ring hollow, especially when we truly do reflect on the evidence nature puts our way. For even if we allow that free will somehow accounts for the miseries humankind suffers, it is hard to see how *our* free will can justify the sufferings and misfortunes that befall other sentient creatures. *They* are hardly responsible for our "original" sin or for any of our other freely chosen misdeeds. The Abrahamic religions evade this problem by insisting that God gave man dominion over the plants and animals he created. Whoever takes this doctrine to heart is inclined to believe that only human suffering matters or, in extreme cases, that only human suffering exists. In recent decades, the dangers inherent in this way of thinking have become increasingly apparent. It has therefore become harder than it used to be to take it seriously.

The Christian doctrine of original sin provides the most extreme version of the blame-the-victim-for-evil strategy.

Adam and Eve, the first man and woman, were expelled from the Garden of Eden because they *freely* chose to disobey God. God then punished them and their descendents until the end of time for this transgression, meting out the afflictions with which humankind would thereafter contend, including death, disease, and burdensome toil. So much retribution is hard to reconcile with a sense of proportionality: How could even the jealous and vengeful God the Bible depicts inflict so momentous a punishment for so slight an infraction? For the Christian Left, and for the Lefts of other religions too, there is an additional problem: they must somehow resist the conclusion that it only continues humanity's original sin to fight back against these divine punishments by struggling to build a new Eden here on fallen earth.

*   *   *

For as long as there has been a distinctively Christian political theory—in other words, from the time that Christianity shed its origins as an otherworldly Jewish sect to become the official religion of Imperial Rome—the story of the fall has been deemed to have far-reaching political implications. Christian thinkers, in need of a political theory suitable for Christianity's new circumstances, developed a philosophy that takes sin—or, as demythologizers might say, human *imperfection* and *insufficiency*—seriously. Their signal contention was that political institutions are necessary evils, not positive goods, the way the Greeks and (pre-Christian) Romans thought they were. Political institutions work *against* human nature; they repress it for the sake of order and peace. Thus Christianity turned Aristotelian political philosophy on its head. For Aristotle, human beings are essentially political animals; participation in politics is therefore indispensable for a fully realized human life. For Christian political thinkers, political institutions are burdens that conflict with the free expression of (fallen) human nature. They are evils; though, compared to alternatives in which they do not exist, necessary and lesser evils.

This profoundly nonclassical sensibility, expressed in symbolic form, holds that the loss of freedom that political institutions bring about is among the punishments God leveled against the descendants of Adam and Eve. But the punishments for original sin are also, ironically, remedies for its consequences. Chief among these punishments is mortality and its concomitant, the fear of violent death. It is this fear that underlies our abhorrence of insecurity and disorder. We are fearful too of losing our possessions, the things of this earth that we have come to love in our postlapsarian condition. Political institutions are able to coordinate individuals' behaviors, mitigating the otherwise devastating consequences of untrammeled expressions of human nature, because these fears make the use or threat of force efficacious. What makes political institutions necessary therefore also makes them possible.

At the dawn of the modern era, Thomas Hobbes recast the Christian understanding of human insufficiency in a materialist and therefore secular framework—imputing innate psychological dispositions to men and women that, left unchecked, would result in the war of all against all that Christian thinkers warned against. Wittingly or not, he demythologized the Christian story. But there is a key aspect of that story that he abandoned. For Christians, a war of all against all is unthinkable because it is inimical to God's plan for saving the elect of all nations through the growth of the church and the administration of its sacraments; God established political institutions to ensure that his will would be done. For Hobbes, the problem was that individuals' interests are poorly served in a state of war in comparison to what would be the case in conditions of peace. Therefore, insofar as they are rational and self-interested, they will avoid this outcome when and insofar as they are able. Hobbes went on to show how this could come to pass through human efforts alone—without any need for divine intervention.

Hobbes's account makes no reference to humanity's theological condition; only to psychological properties that can be described in materialist terms. Nevertheless, it is fair to say that, as much as any Christian thinker, he took sin—or, rather, its secular analogue—seriously. As in the theological account he secularized, Hobbes deemed human beings incapable of doing well for themselves or each other outside coercive structures that prevent them from acting in the ways they are inclined. But, in Hobbes's view, the insufficiencies of human nature are of no consequence for matters of transcendent, immaterial, importance—like the execution of God's plan for his creation or the salvation of souls. What matters is only that individuals, left unconstrained, are unable to realize their interests as well as they otherwise might. This is why reason requires that, when they can, they make themselves unfree— to the extent necessary for peace. In this way, they make outcomes better *for themselves*. In the Christian argument, God, not man, established temporal authorities to further *his* purposes; in Hobbes's version, individuals establish political communities to further *their own*.

There are sins to which we human beings are susceptible in consequence of our fallen condition. In their commission, free will again plays a role, for no evil can be ascribed directly to an omnipotent, omniscient, and perfectly good God. This thought leads to the conclusion that sinners, not their Creator, are responsible for what they do. It also underwrites the distinct, though related, conviction that sinners ought to be held accountable for their actions; especially for their sins—not just in the world to come, but here and now, by the authorities God established.

This inference too is susceptible to a secular reformulation. The political institutions individuals concoct exist to coordinate their behaviors. They do so not only by threatening force but also, when threats fail, by deploying it. That disobedients be held to account, by force if necessary, is therefore in the nature of the institutions rational, self-interested individuals establish. Thus self-interest leads us to move from a state of nature, in which everyone is free to do whatever they please, to an unfree and therefore unnatural, though preferable, *political* condition, in which disobeying the authorities is either impossible or inordinately costly, thanks to the force authorities are able to deploy. Hobbes reasoned that because individuals are relatively equal in the distribution of natural endowments, they can only achieve this result by combining their forces to establish a "common power" that holds them "in awe." That power is the sovereign. Because the sovereign can combine the forces of many, he is mighty enough to be feared and can therefore do what no other individual can—reliably issue enforceable commands.[4] However, his ability to get his commands enforced is artificial. It is not his own powers but the powers of those who have made him their sovereign that makes enforcement possible. The sovereign's power is conventional, not natural. It is also indispensable for avoiding a devastating war of all against all.

Philosophers after Hobbes retained his case for sovereignty and his account of its implications for individual accountability, while restoring the distinction between might and right that Hobbes abandoned. For these philosophers, the fact that some individual or some institutions—governments, for example—are able to issue enforceable commands does not justify their authority; for that, commands must be issued *rightfully*. With this understanding secure, Hobbes's successors went on to moralize the notion of political accountability. When the sovereign commands rightfully, individuals ought to obey for reasons distinct from, though consistent with and complementary to, the prudential reasons Hobbes identified. Therefore, when subjects fail to obey, they are morally, not just politically, accountable.

In joining a notion of rightfulness to a Hobbesian understanding of the need for political authority, Hobbes's successors set in motion changes equally momentous. Chief among them is the extension of the idea of accountability into the domain of distributive justice. For those who believe that human beings are *morally* responsible for what they freely choose to do, a natural inference is that, insofar as institutions are properly responsive to free choices, individuals *deserve* what they get. This contention does not strictly imply a view about what a just distribution of benefits and burdens should be because it leaves unsettled how much of an individual's distributive share is deserved. One could argue, for example, that because market generated distributions mainly or entirely reflect luck, not free choice, individuals deserve none of what market systems deal them—even if there are compelling reasons, other than how deserving they are, for them to keep some or all of their market-generated shares. One could even go so far as to hold that in principle nothing can be deserved because no choices are genuinely free.

Christianity is equivocal on issues of desert. After the fall, no one deserves anything except eternal torment. But there is also a sense in which individuals do deserve what becomes theirs through the normal operations of established institutional arrangements. Since the institutions that distribute benefits and burdens are divinely established, their consequences should be respected. This equivocation attaches to attitudes toward poverty and wealth. Jesus said that it is more difficult for the rich to enter into the kingdom of heaven than for a camel to pass through the eye of a needle.[5] Perhaps. But in the meanwhile, it is wrong to intervene to correct for the extraworldly "misfortune" the well-off of this world may confront on Judgment Day. The rich accept this conclusion with equanimity. Even if they are not "atheists without knowing it," they are sensible enough to want their pie here on earth—not in God's heaven. Religious authorities seldom gainsay them.

Thus the Christian response to the argument from evil underwrites a chain of thought that supports inequality.

The Christian—and, more generally, Abrahamic—response to the argument from evil also touches on notions of fraternity (community). One would suppose that when human beings are variously afflicted, whether or not it is their own fault, their fellow human beings would, in solidarity, come to their aid. But if we take to heart the idea that individuals' lots are deserved, the motivation to come to the aid of others is attenuated. This is not to say that the Abrahamic religions counsel indifference. But insofar as they discourage solidarity, they encourage acceptance of conditions that leave individuals on their own as they face the world and each other. In this respect, too, the Abrahamic religions sustain modes of thinking that tend in the opposite direction from those that the political Left has always favored. What the one fosters, the other militates against.

In place of solidarity, the Abrahamic religions counsel "love"—the kind the fathers of the church called *caritas*, charity. Here, again, the Christian position is especially revealing, though similar notions are at work in all the Abrahamic faiths. They all acknowledge a duty to relieve suffering and they all hold that this duty applies to the suffering poverty causes. For Roman Catholics, it is saintly to work among the poor and to share their fate; many Protestant sects advance similar views, along with Muslims and Jews. However, relieving poverty on a case-by-case basis does not amount to a strategy for ending poverty. Jesus taught that "the poor will always be with us."[6] It is a good thing, for those who follow his

teaching, that this is so because poverty provides opportuni-
ties for exercising *caritas*. Christians who believe in salvation
through works can help themselves by helping others, and
those who subscribe to the more orthodox view that salvation
only comes through unmerited grace can put the poverty of
others to similar use. For them, the exercise of *caritas* is a
symptom, not a cause, of being saved. Therefore, if they act
charitably, *as if* they are among the elect, they can find it
easier to believe that they really are. Relieving the poverty of
others can therefore help them relieve anxiety about their lot
in eternity.

Needless to say, an omnipotent, omniscient, and perfectly
good God could eliminate poverty, should he choose. Even
human beings can. We have succeeded, or at least come close,
in comparatively rich countries where Left, usually social
democratic, policies prevailed. What was required was a high,
but attainable, level of economic development and sound
redistributive policies. Global poverty poses graver challenges. But were its elimination a priority, it should be possible to make considerable headway. Poverty is no longer
inevitable, as it was in Biblical times. Thanks to economic
development, it is eliminable, if not immediately everywhere,
then everywhere in an already foreseeable future—provided
there is the political will. Wittingly or not, those who hold fast
to the idea that exercising charity by working with the poor
will be an obligation until the end of time must therefore
believe that God *wants* poverty to endure—that it is part of
his design, and therefore that it is good in some inscrutable
way that so many suffer as they do.

But this is nonsense. In precapitalist societies, poverty was mainly a consequence of endemic scarcity. In developed countries, where there is wealth enough to implement egalitarian distributions at a high level, it is a by-product of socially constructed and therefore changeable institutional arrangements. To be sure, as with the phenomena Durkheim sought to explain sociologically, there is always a story to tell about why particular individuals are poor; one that does not directly implicate social facts. But the fact that so many are poor has social, not individual, causes. So too does the global division between rich and poor. These deplorable and unnecessary conditions are consequences of the system in place. They can no more be explained by compiling explanations for the poverty of particular individuals or countries than individuals' behaviors can be explained by conjoining explanations for all the chemical reactions in their bodies. Poverty is a social phenomenon that social and political factors explain and that political transformations can rectify.

Christianity and the other Abrahamic religions are, at best, ambivalent about poverty. Like God's love for his creation, human love for the wretched of the earth is not only compatible with suffering; it requires it. If evils did not exist, it would be impossible for we humans, made in God's image, to act *in imitatio Deo*, in imitation of God. The Left has always had a different idea. It has never tried to imitate the incalculably cruel love emanating from an allegedly perfect being, but to correct for his sadism or incompetence or both.

*　　*　　*

Along with liberty and equality, fraternity (community) is an integral part of the Left *Gestalt*. For the Abrahamic religions community is constituted by belief or rather, since the emphasis on belief is largely an artifact of Christianity's influence, identification with coreligionists. The *ummah*, the (global) Muslim community, is a transnational, transethnic fellowship. Judaism evinces a similar, though less universalistic, notion. Before the word was appropriated by Zionists and made the name of an ethnocratic settler-state, "Israel" designated all Jewish believers, regardless of their places of residence or citizenship. In most Christian sects, communities are comprised of like-thinking congregations. When these communities are small, as in some Protestant denominations, the notion approximates the genuine article. Otherwise, it is without content. This is even more plainly the case when Christendom, the "community" of all Christians, is invoked. Still, it has become plain in recent years that the idea of Christendom continues to resonate even in secular Europe, whenever Islam, Christianity's arch rival of centuries past, appears to threaten. But this is the weakest imaginable sort of "community." More generally, in all the Abrahamic religions, a sense of community can be and typically has been passive to the point of notional; it is not clear what, if any, obligations community membership entails. In certain times and places, historical contingencies invest ties to coreligionists with special importance. However, even in exceptional circumstances, it takes a great deal for Abrahamic "communities" to evince active expressions of unity, much less of fraternity in the modern sense.

Moreover in a world in which religions compete, the pertinent notion of community, whatever its salience, is at odds with expressions of universal human solidarity that cross boundaries between peoples. The crusading spirit may have originated in Christian conditions for reasons that at least partly transcend matters of belief. But the basic idea—in-group solidarity and its inevitable consequence, hostility to outsiders—is endemic to all the Abrahamic faiths. It is a small step, frequently made, between out-group hostility and the gruesome atrocities human beings perpetrate against one another in the name of their God.

Real fraternity implies solidarity—unity of purpose and effect, based on experiential social bonds. To act in *solidarity* with an individual or group is to support the endeavors of others either symbolically or at some personal or collective cost or both. It requires that we deliberate and act in full acknowledgement of our commonalities with others; that we identify with our fellow human beings across space and time and regardless of doctrinal commitments or accidents of birth. This is not to say that the ideal requires that everyone regard everyone else in the same way. Even were it desirable to do so, that would be humanly impossible for most people most of the time. But it is not desirable. Universal human solidarity is not only consistent with but actually requires special regard for family, friends, and other intimates, and indeed for the entire web of social identifications that cluster, as if in concentric circles, around each person. The paradigm is relations between brothers, fraternity. The idea is not to obliterate this primordial solidarity, but to extend it, in appropriate ways and degrees, to everyone; to forge a brotherhood of human beings as such.

*　　*　　*

The *Gestalt* comprised of liberty, equality, and fraternity militates against systemic animosities. The Abrahamic religions do the opposite. They encourage out-group hostilities. By acquiescing to prevailing inequalities of income and wealth and by offering longstanding and continuing support for prevailing hierarchies and inequalities of status, they also encourage internal strife. The problem is obviously more than just the disingenuous invocation of free will. But this is the root of the problem; it is what encourages the Abrahamic faiths to regard existing inequalities and restrictions on freedom as deserved. On this rock, an enormous conservative superstructure has arisen—responsible for countless past and present horrors and now, with increasingly lethal powers available to those in the grip of faith, threatening even worse in the future.

This is why a religious Left is an unstable configuration. It may be and often is psychologically possible for the faithful to promote liberty, equality, and fraternity; it is the human lot to embrace contradictory positions and to be internally conflicted. But, as Feuerbach understood, emancipation depends on overcoming this ambivalence politically—on developing a politics consistent with a clear and unambivalent understanding of what God is or, rather, *is not*. In the political sphere, if not in individuals' hearts and minds, modes of thinking, feeling, and being that incline in opposite directions cannot indefinitely coexist. Of these competing *Gestalten*, one leads, as it were, to war and Armageddon; the other to the city of God, the heavenly fortress. Those who find these designations meaningful are right about what the options are. But their understanding of what they involve desperately needs to be set aright because, as Feuerbach also realized, what they envision is a metaphorical inversion of what is really the case. The city of God, demythologized, represents what is humanly possible once the God illusion is overcome. So long as that illusion and the ways of thinking it sustains degrade political life, Armageddon or rather its demythologized functional equivalent, unending strife for the sake of convictions held at first in ignorance and now in bad faith, remains a live and profoundly menacing prospect.

*   *   *

Thus, in the end, we return to where we began: with Young Hegelian atheism—not because it is the last word, but because it is the next word for those still en route to transcending faith altogether.

Feuerbach was right to insist that for human beings to establish Heaven on earth they must take consciousness of a deep truth: that what the Abrahamic religions promise is neither more nor less than what is *humanly* possible. Feuerbach also insisted that the task of everyone who understands this is to work to actualize the possibilities the Abrahamic religions "invert"—in other words, to do "God's work." What those religions depict as a "gift" bestowed upon a fortunate few by an omnipotent, omniscient, and perfectly good God is in reality humanity's historical mission. Facing that reality squarely, without illusions, is an indispensable step in carrying it forward.

The men and women who comprise the religious Left understand this, at the same time that they do not, so to speak, understand that they do. Those who identify with God and also with liberty, equality, and fraternity put their faith to work in ways that may seem coherent to themselves and to others. They do so, however, by deceiving themselves about what they dare not acknowledge—that they have placed their trust in an illusion, an unconscious and, in this case, an unreasonable desire. Moreover, the illusion that inspires them is not politically innocent; it is associated, historically and conceptually, with everything they oppose.

For those on the religious Left to overcome bad faith and, more importantly, to militate unequivocally on the side of forces working to put the world on a surer, more progressive track, it is urgent that they cognize their faith correctly, and project its affect onto what truly elicits it. Shorn of the metaphysical carapace that renders the Young Hegelian corpus all but inaccessible to anyone not immersed in the history of German thought, this is what the Young Hegelians can still teach us. What moved them—and what can move us still—was a sense of the need to transform faith in God into faith in humanity, so that real world men and women can rectify human causes of human misery to the greatest possible extent. There is no other way to make life meaningful again in face of the death of the Abrahamic God.

CONCLUSION

I t soon became clear that, notwithstanding the advances it brought in its wake, the French Revolution, which was supposed to have set humanity on the path to real freedom, had not ushered in anything like heaven on earth. A few dauntless and enlightened thinkers wondered why. One reason, they all agreed, was resistance on nearly everyone's part to enlightenment itself. Feuerbach, Durkheim, Freud, and Nietzsche were among those who tried to account for this resistance—in general and with regard to the Abrahamic religions, which, they all assumed, would have vanished like night into day had enlightened thinking prevailed. Their explanations for faith's persistence differ along many dimensions but, notwithstanding these differences, they point in a similar direction: ascribing theism's durability to a universal human need to find meaning in a meaningless world. On this point, they were surely right. Nevertheless, their respective explanations, separately and together, are incomplete and far from satisfactory. Still, theirs are the most illuminating attempts at explaining theism's persistence to date. Future investigators—drawing on more contemporary, probably sounder, science—will do well to study these thinkers' efforts to make sense of senseless convictions, and to take what they can from them. My main interest has been to tease a normative standard, proper to enlightened thinking, out of their work and to show how, in relation to that standard, contemporary theism stands indicted. I have concluded, on this basis, that, for almost everyone in the world today, Abrahamic faith is bad faith. This is not the only thing wrong with the opium of the people in the early years of the twenty-first century, but it is a damning reproach. It applies to all modern believers—including those whose faith is comparatively benign and even to those for whom faith motivates good works and, remarkably, good politics.

It has been plain for a long time what ought to happen: the Abrahamic religions should go the way of the pagan faiths that preceded them. Thanks to Feuerbach, Durkheim, Freud, and Nietzsche, we also have some idea of why this has not yet occurred; and, implicitly, why it is reprehensible that faith lingers. Feuerbach expressly, and the other authors implicitly, also advanced a suggestion about how to get from where we now are to where we ought to be. Feuerbach was the most explicit but they all thought that all would be well when and insofar as people put reason in control. That suggestion reflects the inherent optimism of enlightened thinking, even at its most pessimistic—in Freud's account of civilization's discontents. Enlightened thinkers expect a great deal from enlightenment itself; too much, perhaps.

But reason does not have to be in control for faith to subside. For most people, progress towards enlightened ends depends less on reason winning hearts and minds than on sheer, but beneficent, indifference. Where secularism has made headway, it has not been, for the most part, because people became atheists first (or ever), but because, for reasons specific to particular times and places, faith came to seem unimportant to them; because they lost interest and therefore drifted away from religious identifications and "faith perspectives." This has happened gradually in most of Europe for more than half a century; there are signs that it is currently taking place at a more rapid pace in sectors of the American population, especially among the young. If so, this would be all for the good. But it is not what enlightened thinkers imagined would happen. Their expectation was that reason would triumph frontally; not that unreason would be defeated in a protracted war of attrition. Too bad for that expectation! If the forward march not of reason but of indifference gets us from here to there, then so be it.

Of course, at the same time that secularism advances inexorably, there is the countervailing phenomenon of regression—where peoples in the grip of bad faith and caring not all that much about what drove their ancestors to ruinous distraction revert to pre-enlightened levels of religious fervor. Are we at the threshold of a new religious "awakening"? There are parts of the world where it might seem so, and nowhere is entirely immune. But since the most affected quarters of the planet are those where imperialist depredations are at their most virulent, I think that, for this unfortunate turn of events, we have mainly global politics to thank. I would venture that what we are witnessing is an outbreak of a wrong-headed but copiously motivated resistance to domination, an anti-imperialism of fools. We will only know for sure in the fullness of time. But if I am right, Young Hegelian optimism may well find more vindication among peoples now moving backwards than among those whose less harmful bad faith is shallower. For within subaltern groups moved by highly politicized versions of traditional religious teachings, all that is needed is a salutary "taking consciousness" of the real meaning of their militancy. Positivists and (Hegelian) negativists may be right in thinking that all of humankind will succeed in establishing a godless future somehow, someday. Paradoxically, it may be that the descendants of those who are now the least enlightened among us will lead the way.

In any case, it is urgent that we arrive at transparency, that we allow God to rest in peace—and the sooner this comes to pass, the better. We all either do know or ought to know that God is dead. The time is past due to come to terms with this awareness. As Feuerbach foretold, there is no other way for our long-suffering species to beat down the gates of heaven in order to become truly free.

NOTES

PREFACE

1. I discuss Althusserian and analytical Marxism in *A Future for Marxism?: Althusser, the Analytical Turn and the Revival of Socialist Theory* (London: Pluto Press, 2003).

2. See my *Engaging Political Philosophy: From Hobbes to Rawls* (Malden, MA: Blackwell Publishers, 2002).

INTRODUCTION

1. I use the masculine pronoun rather than "she" or "it" because, notwithstanding recent efforts to feminize or degender the concept, the God of Abraham, Isaac, and Jacob remains profoundly and ineluctably patriarchal, and it is well to keep this evident truth plainly in mind.

2. See, for example, Todd Tremlin, *Minds and Gods: The Cognitive Foundations of Religion* (Oxford: Oxford University Press, 2006).

3. *Summa Theologica*, Part One, Question II, Third Article.

4. For reasons I will presently explain, the first four are "cosmological" arguments, the last is a "teleological" argument.

5. This formulation owes to the German philosopher Gottfried Wilhelm Leibniz (1646–1716). On his account, the Principle of Sufficient Reason is, along with the Law of Non-Contradiction, a core principle of intelligibility.

6. According to *Modus Ponens*, "if x, then y" and "x" imply "y." Let "x" stand for "God exists in the understanding," and let "y" stand for "God exists in reality." Then, Anselm's argument goes: "if God exists in the understanding, then God exists in reality"; "God exists in the understanding" therefore, by the rule *Modus Ponens*, "God exists in reality." The inference is beyond dispute and even atheists would have to agree that the second premise, "x," that "God exists in the understanding," is true; otherwise they could not deny "y," that "God exists in reality." Therefore, the soundness of the argument depends on the truth of its first premise—the conditional sentence "if x, then y"—that "if God exists in the understanding, then he exists in reality." On this reconstruction of Anselm's case for God's existence, what analysis of the concept of God is supposed to reveal is the truth of this premise.

7. G. E. Moore, "Is Existence a Predicate?" *Aristotelian Society*, Supplementary Volume 15 (1936), pp. 175–88. This paper is available in many anthologies.

8. Any two things are alike in *some* respects; therefore it is always possible to hold that what is true of one is, by analogy, true of the other. But the strength of the inference depends on the strength of the analogy. The parts of nature to which proponents of the argument from design appeal are, like Nature itself, sufficiently *unlike* objects that we know to be designed, objects of human contrivance, that inferences based on their similarities will always be dubious at best.

9. See David Hume, *Dialogues Concerning Natural Religion* (1779), especially the interventions of the character Philo in part 8. Unlike the hypothesis of a Godly designer, the randomness hypothesis does at least lend itself to a naturalistic interpretation. If the ancient Greek atomists and their modern successors were right, the world is comprised of independent atoms pursuing random motions. Then,

presumably, these atoms will frequently collide, causing them to go their separate ways. But in the fullness of time, some stable configurations are bound to coalesce. Because only what is stable can survive, what we observe will seem orderly and therefore designed. Arguably, then, the evidence proponents of teleological arguments adduce supports the hypothesis that chance rules the world at least as well as it supports the hypothesis that a designer does.

One could argue too that the development of "chaos theory," a branch of mathematics unknown in the eighteenth and nineteenth centuries, lends additional support to the chance hypothesis—making it, if anything, more probable than the design hypothesis. Chaos theory demonstrates how order can emerge out of disorder (chaos).

10. See William James, *The Varieties of Religious Experience*, first published 1902.

CHAPTER ONE: ATHEISM: YOUNG HEGELIAN STYLE

1. For a collection of Young Hegelian writings, see Lawrence S. Stepelevich, ed., *The Young Hegelians: An Anthology* (Prometheus Books, 1997). For general accounts of the movement, see William J. Brazill, *The Young Hegelians* (New Haven: Yale University Press, 1970); Warren Breckman, *Marx, the Young Hegelians, and the Origins of Radical Social Theory: Dethroning the Self* (Cambridge: Cambridge University Press, 1999); "Feuerbach, Marx and the Left Hegelians," special issue of *The Philosophical Forum* 8, nos. 2–4 (1978); Sidney Hook, *From Hegel to Marx: Studies in the Intellectual Development of Karl Marx* (Ann Arbor: University of Michigan Press, originally published 1936); Stathis Kouvelakis, *Philosophy and Revolution: From Kant to Marx*, trans. G. M. Goshgarian (London: Verso, 2003); Harold

Mah, *The End of Philosophy, the Origin of "Ideology": Karl Marx and the Crisis of the Young Hegelians* (Berkeley: University of California Press, 1987); Karl Löwith, *From Hegel to Nietzsche: The Revolution in Nineteenth Century Thought*, trans. David E. Green (Garden City, NY: Anchor Books, 1967; original German edition 1941); and David McLellan, *The Young Hegelians and Karl Marx* (New York: F. A. Praeger, 1969).

2. Ludwig Feuerbach, *The Essence of Christianity* (Amherst, NY: Prometheus Books, 1989). Originally published 1841.

3. Decades after the Young Hegelian movement expired, Marxists made the term "dialectical materialism" their own. It then took on meanings that should not be confounded with the configuration of positions that Feuerbach set out to develop. Some Marxists used the term to designate sets of doctrines that functioned as quasiofficial dogmas in Communist countries. The term was also used as a synonym for "Marxist philosophy." What is intended here, however, is only what the words say: a dialectical materialism is a (post-Cartesian) materialism that imputes a (Hegelian) dialectical structure to matter.

4. Marx was emphatic on this point in his *Theses on Feuerbach* and in *The German Ideology* (1845).

5. In discussing Feuerbach, this ostensibly gendered designation is sometimes unavoidable—not, as is the case of God, because the concept "man" (*Mensch*), as Feuerbach understood it, is inherently patriarchal, but because there is no gender neutral word in English or German or any other language (so far as I know) that felicitously replaces it, and because it is sometimes better to use a masculine term than a clumsy or evasive circumlocution.

6. Immanuel Kant, *The Critique of Pure Reason*, B, II, "Of the Ideal of the Summum Bonum as a Determining Ground of the Ultimate End of Pure Reason."

7. In addition to *The Critique of Pure Reason*, there is also *The Critique of Practical Reason* (1788) and *The Critique of Judgment* (1790).

8. The expression occurs in the opening paragraphs of the 1843 "Introduction" to "The Critique of Hegel's *Philosophy of Right*."

9. In Marx's hands, Hegel's account of the *Rechtstaat* and then the findings of British political economists were at the top of the list. Thus the Young Hegelian writings for which Marx is best known are "The Critique of Hegel's *Philosophy of Right*" (1843) and the (1844) *Economic and Philosophic Manuscripts* (sometimes called the *Paris Manuscripts*).

10. The expression occurs in the "Introduction" to "The Critique of Hegel's *Philosophy of Right*."

11. As the 1840s unfolded, most Young Hegelians, Marx especially, came to identify the revolutionary agent with the nascent industrial proletariat. Feuerbach's own conception was more diffuse. For Marx's first clear enunciation of the proletariat's historical mission, see ibid.

12. See ibid. The expression "opium of the people" and the words that precede it occur in the opening paragraphs of that text.

13. The slogan "pessimism of the intellect, optimism of the will" appeared regularly on the masthead of the journal Gramsci established, *Ordine Nuovo*.

14. "Wiser" because the strongest case for theism, the so-called argument from design, according to which the evidence of nature is supposed to support the hypothesis that God exists in the way that evidence supports hypotheses generally, provides better support for the existence of the spiteful and mean-spirited "powers" of ancient mythologies than for a perfect being.

CHAPTER TWO: A SOCIAL THING

1. Nowhere is this point more influentially asserted than in John Rawls, *Political Liberalism* (New York: Columbia University Press, 1993). See especially Lecture VI (pp. 212–54), "The Idea of Public Reason."

2. William James, *The Varieties of Religious Experience*, first published 1902.

3. For contemporary philosophers, *holism* designates a weaker, though related, position, according to which evidence corroborates or infirms entire theories rather than specific claims within them. The idea is that there is no strict 'correspondence' between propositions and facts, but rather between theories and the world they purport to account for. Hegel's holism was more far-reaching. For him, there are no discrete theories, but only one true explanation of everything or, more precisely, of everything "real." Everything else, the "merely apparent," may also be explainable in some sense. But these explanations have nothing to do with what is ultimately real and therefore have no place in Hegel's account.

4. *Elementary Forms*, pp. 34–35.

5. Ibid., p. 2: "Fundamentally, then, there are no religions that are false. All are true after their own fashion: All fulfill given conditions of human existence, though in different ways. . . ."

6. As remarked in chapter one, Kant's defense of empirical knowledge is the prototype. To combat skepticism, Kant set out to show what must be the case for experience to be real. He then, independently, showed how these conditions follow from the nature of reason itself.

7. Endogenous developmental logics can govern more or less strictly inasmuch as it is one thing to identify such processes and something else to say that they explain what actually happens. The

difference arises because there can be exogenous, countervailing factors that block what would otherwise be "historically inevitable." For example, Marx's theory of history, historical materialism, identifies a process that moves history along from one epochal stage to another. The idea, roughly, is that economic structures (combinations of "forces" and "relations" of production) change discontinuously to track increasingly higher levels of development of productive forces. But factors outside the theory's range can and do affect the process Marx identified; they could even derail it permanently. Thus historical materialism only explains what would happen *ceteris absentibus*, in the absence of other causes. As such, it can be and often is enlightening, even if it seldom or never explains the epochal historical transformations it purports to account for. In contrast, Comte's account of history's trajectory is only descriptive. It is not a theory of what *would* happen *ceteris absentibus*, but an account of what has happened. In retrospect, it is always possible to supply a "Whiggish" or "one thing leads to another" rationale for the way things have gone. That rationale can even be extrapolated to apply outside areas where there is direct evidence—as Durkheim did, to the extent that he assumed that the Abrahamic and other world religions were preceded by forms of religious life similar to those still observable among aboriginal peoples. But conjecturing on "natural" chains of development is different from identifying endogenous processes. The most one can conclude, on the former basis, is that it is likely that development has proceeded (or will proceed) in a certain way. On the latter basis, one is entitled to say that development *will* proceed in a certain way, unless "exogenous" factors interfere.

8. See Claude Lèvi-Strauss, *Le totemisme aujourd'hui* (1962). Translated by Rodney Needham, *Totemism* (1963).

9. However, Judaism's commitment to the idea has been tenuous at certain moments of its history. Among non-Abrahamic

world religions, the Buddhist position is more nuanced than most in the sense that, for Buddhism, the soul is ultimately unreal and therefore, when fully realized, *nothing*. In this sense, Buddhists deny that there are souls. Nevertheless, there is a sense in which souls exist for Buddhists too, and not just in popular versions of Buddhism. How else can we understand the claim that souls are reincarnated countless times as they proceed along the path to ultimate annihilation? It appears that Buddhism took over a popular belief and then transformed it radically, but without discarding its constituent ideas altogether. If Buddhism is indeed a nontheistic religion, as Durkheim maintained, it did much the same with the idea of gods. Nearly all strains of Buddhist thought invoke gods, many of them of pre-Buddhist origin, in their lore and in traditional forms of worship. But Buddhism does not countenance anything like the Abrahamic belief in an omnipotent, omniscient, perfectly good being with whom human beings can enter into personal relationships.

10. The Abrahamic religions, because they support the Creation story found in the opening chapters of Genesis, according to which God created everything out of nothing, are committed to the idea that whatever now exists must at some past time have come into existence. Therefore, earlier still (whatever that might mean), it did not exist at all. One of the consequences of Abrahmic dominance over the prevailing intellectual culture is that this notion—of creation *ex nihilo,* from nothing—has entered into common sense and become deeply entrenched there. However, for most of the world's peoples, including the peoples of Greco-Roman antiquity and their philosophers, the idea of creation *ex nihilo* is absurd. For them, if there are souls now, there must always have been souls or else souls must come from something that existed before them. Abrahamic religions are vague on this point but they seem to maintain that, although existing souls survive for all eternity, they arose

at a determinate moment in time—when the persons to whom they are attached were conceived, or at "quickening" (shortly after conception) or, in less benighted versions, at birth.

11. Durkheim discusses this process at length in chapters eight and nine of *Elementary Forms of Religious Life.*

CHAPTER THREE: THE TENACITY OF AN ILLUSION

1. See, especially, Sigmund Freud, *Civilization and Its Discontents* (1930).

2. Descartes was certainly wrong about rational theology and therefore, in light of his strategy for defending the new sciences of nature, about science too. In *Meditation* 3, he used one of the "clear and distinct" ideas the *I* has, the idea of a perfect being, to argue, by means of a cosmological argument, that "God exists." His argument is dubious for many reasons, not least the general one sketched above in the introduction. In *Meditation* 5, Descartes advanced an ontological argument that is similarly unsatisfactory. Inasmuch as one of Descartes's aims was to defend theism, he had reason to regret the failure of rational theology in its own right. What is worse for Descartes, though, is that the failure of rational theology undoes his attempt to establish that science is about the real. Descartes was able to make that claim by arguing that, since we can know that God exists, we can know that there is a perfectly good (truthful) being who guarantees the veracity of our clear and distinct ideas—by which he meant, at this stage of his argument, ideas that are susceptible to mathematical representation in the manner of the new sciences. God therefore guarantees that science is about the real; in other words, his existence vanquishes the possibility that an evil demon is deceiving us with respect to the apparent certain-

ties science reveals. But if God's existence cannot be established, then, in light of how Descartes's strategy unfolds, there is no guarantee; and Descartes's attempt to defeat skepticism fails.

3. See chapter two. In *Suicide* (first published 1897), Durkheim conceded that behind every suicide, there is an individual-level (psychological) story to tell; and therefore a psychological explanation. But, he argued nevertheless that there is no way in principle to explain differential suicide rates by conjoining these stories together. That social fact requires a distinctively social explanation.

4. See, for example, *Five Lectures on Psychoanalysis* (1910) and, among many other writings of Freud's, *Beyond the Pleasure Principle* (1920).

5. Well-known proponents of this view include Wilhelm Reich and Herbert Marcuse. See, for example, Reich, *Character Analysis* (1933) and Marcuse, *Eros and Civilization* (1955).

6. See chapter three and especially chapter eight, the concluding chapter, of *Civilization and Its Discontents*.

7. See Todd Tremlin, *Minds and Gods: The Cognitive Foundations of Religion* (Oxford: Oxford University Press, 2006).

8. However, Freud was plainly interested in this question from a historical point of view. In a very late work, *Moses and Monotheism* (1939), he advanced several contentious claims—arguing, among other things, that monotheism was an Egyptian invention and that Moses was Egyptian, not Israelite.

9. Evolution is an improver only in this very attenuated sense; it is an improver relative to particular environmental conditions. The more fit "survive" by out-reproducing the less fit. This is why it is misleading to maintain, as Social Darwinists did, that Darwinian theory establishes "the survival of the fittest." From a Darwinian perspective, wherever natural selection accounts for evolutionary change, "the survival of the fittest" is a tautology; it has no deeper

significance—and no normative force. Natural selection explains myriad small-scale changes. Cumulatively, these changes may increase complexity. But this is not its point. Darwinian theory acknowledges no "higher" end in view, no pregiven *telos*; and certainly no inevitable evolutionary trajectory from single-celled organisms to human beings and then to the kinds of human beings that Social Darwinists esteemed.

10. *Civilization and Its Discontents*, chapter one.

11. James, *Varieties of Religious Experience*.

CHAPTER FOUR: BEYOND GOD AND EVIL

1. See Immanuel Kant, "What is Enlightenment?" (1784).

2. This contention, developed originally by French postmodernists is best known in the English-speaking world thanks to the work of the late Richard Rorty. See, for example, Richard Rorty, *Philosophy and the Mirror of Nature* (Princeton, NJ: Princeton University Press, 1981) and *Contingency, Irony and Solidarity* (Cambridge: Cambridge University Press, 1989).

3. Even more than God Himself, Nietzsche's "superman" was gendered male. Whether or not he "really" meant it, Nietzsche's writings are misogynistic and, more even than the Abrahamic religions, beyond feminist reconstruction.

4. "How One Philosophizes with a Hammer" was the subtitle Nietzsche gave to *The Twilight of the Idols (Götzen-Dämmerung)* (written in 1888, first published in 1889). The title is a pun on the title of Richard Wagner's opera, *Götterdämmerung* or "Twilight of the Gods."

5. Kant's account of the reasoning leading to the notion of a categorical imperative and his various formulations of the idea can

be found in parts I and II of *The Groundwork of the Metaphysics of Morals* (1785).

6. That the future is open was a recurrent theme in Nietzsche's writings. The aphorisms that comprise the fifth and final section of *The Gay Science* (1882) make this point with particular eloquence and clarity.

7. The principle source for Aristotle's ethical views is *The Nichomachean Ethics*. That text is compiled of lectures and other teachings delivered towards the middle and end of the fourth century BCE.

8. See, for example, Friedrich Nietzsche, *The Gay Science*, pp. 120, 382.

9. See Friedrich Nietzsche, *On the Genealogy of Morals* (1887) and also Friedrich Nietzsche, *Beyond Good and Evil* (1886).

10. This is the central theme of Kant's so-called third critique (after *The Critique of Pure Reason* and *The Critique of Practical Reason*), *The Critique of Judgment* (1790).

11. Nietzsche, *Gay Science*, p. 290.

12. See, for example, the first essay of *On the Genealogy of Morals*.

13. See the account of lordship and bondage in *The Phenomenology of Spirit* (1806), part B (Self-Consciousness), section A, pp. 228–40.

14. *On the Genealogy of Morals*, trans. Walter Kaufmann (New York: Vintage, 1989), first essay, no. 14, pp. 46–47

15. The third, concluding essay in *The Genealogy of Morals* is an extensive critique of "the ascetic ideal," but the theme resonates throughout Nietzsche's work. Thus the "science" of the future envisioned in *The Gay Science* contrasts with the portentous, overly serious *ascetic* science of our not-yet-entirely enlightened time.

16. Matthew 5:5. The formulation recounted by Matthew is based on the Psalm 37:11.

17. John Dewey, *The Quest for Certainty: A Study of the Relation of Knowledge and Action* (1929).

18. All the major pragmatists advanced this view but perhaps the clearest defense of it occurs in chapter 30 of William James's *Pragmatism: A New Name For Some Old Ways of Thinking* (1907). The chapter is entitled "The Pragmatic Theory of Truth."

19. See Aristotle, *Nicomachean Ethics*, Book V.

CHAPTER FIVE: THE LIBERAL TURN

1. Edmund Gibbon, *The Decline and Fall of the Roman Empire* (1776), vol. 1, chapter 2.

2. See Max Weber, "Politics as a Vocation," in Hans Gerth and C. Wright Mills, eds., *From Max Weber: Essays in Sociology* (New York: Routledge, 2007).

3. Needless to say, a Hobbesian sovereign, like God himself, is always gendered male.

CHAPTER SIX: A PRECARIOUS LEFT

1. The term "fraternity," derived from the Latin word for brother, has a masculine register. This will suggest to many readers that the idea it articulates is inherently patriarchal. This would be a mistaken inference, but to avoid the problem, I will, when appropriate, use the gender-neutral word "community" interchangeably with "fraternity." However, "community" and "fraternity" are not exactly synonymous—because "community" can be interpreted in ways that "fraternity" cannot.

2. There is an analogy with the way we commonly use words

like "damn." Strictly speaking, to damn is to place a curse—and, in so doing, to venture into a supernatural, though not necessarily theistic, frame of reference. But the term seldom has that connotation nowadays. Whatever the sociopsychological functions of "cursing" may be, placing curses on others—or believing that one is doing so—is seldom among them.

3. Neither Christianity nor any other religious tradition speaks unequivocally or with only one voice. In addition, as one would expect of modes of thought that have endured virtually without opposition for millennia, wherever religious leaders propose simple answers, subtle thinkers complicate the story in countless ways. What is presented here is an unsubtle, but adequate, account of what can fairly be called the consensus view.

4. Hobbes never doubted that the individual who would become sovereign would be male; hence, in this instance too, the appropriateness of the masculine pronoun.

5. Matthew 19:24.

6. Matthew 26:11.